D1373583

What People Are Saying about Susan K. Williams Smith and *Rest for the Justice-Seeking Soul*:

In *Rest for the Justice-Seeking Soul*, Rev. Dr. Susan K. Smith provides a deep pool of wellness and rejuvenation for those who yearn for freedom. Through these inspiring meditations, leaders of all sorts—people working in congregations, organizations, and grassroots communities around the country—will laugh, reflect, and ultimately be restored. If you are feeling "weary and heavy-laden," make sure you purchase this book!

—*Joshua DuBois*
Former White House advisor to President Barack Obama
CNN commentator; CEO, Values Partnerships

Rev. Susan K. Williams Smith's work is a revitalizing jolt to the heart and balm for the soul for those who are active in movements toward collective liberation. It's a must-read for those on the cusp of burnout in the struggle for justice.

—*Rev. Jennifer Butler*
Founding CEO, Faith in Public Life

Justice seekers, friends of the beloved community, come, taste, eat and drink the deep, divine wisdom within these pages—written for you so you might be spiritually nourished and inspired for the work before you. Blending biblical Scripture with stories about justice seekers from a beautiful range of backgrounds, Dr. Susan K. Williams Smith has created a life-giving book that will sustain those who are seeking new sources of strength in this challenging time. Whether you know it or not, you need this book.

—*Rev. Paul Brandeis Raushenbush*
Senior vice president and editor, *Voices*
Auburn Seminary

Susan K. Smith knows what it means to stand in the center of the storm with hurting and struggling people. What does one need to do to hold on to the courage to be fully human in a world that punishes humanity and vulnerability? How does a leader stay grounded and balanced in the throes of a chaotic world? What does it mean for the weary and grieving leader to let God be God? Offered up from the wellspring of her own experiences, faithfulness, and wisdom, *Rest for the Justice-Seeking Soul* reaches deep into the places of the hearts of people who refuse to disengage or live in denial with exactly what our hearts need—daily—to weather difficult times and spaces: encouragement, prodding, challenge, laughter, hope, insight, balm, and grace.

—*Rev. Dr. Emma Jordan-Simpson*
Executive director, Fellowship of Reconciliation USA

SUSAN K. WILLIAMS SMITH

REST FOR THE JUSTICE SEEKING SOUL

90 MEDITATIONS

WHITAKER
HOUSE

REST FOR THE JUSTICE-SEEKING SOUL

Crazyfaithministries.org
Cassady2euca@icloud.com

ISBN: 978-1-64123-308-8
eBook ISBN: 978-1-64123-309-5
Printed in the United States of America
© 2019 by Susan K. Williams Smith

Whitaker House
1030 Hunt Valley Circle
New Kensington, PA 15068
www.whitakerhouse.com

Library of Congress Control Number: 2019947929

1 2 3 4 5 6 7 8 9 10 11 🅌🅙 26 25 24 23 22 21 20 19

CONTENTS

DAY 1

THE QUEST TO "HOPE" SOMEBODY

Seek the LORD and live, or he will break out against the house of Joseph like fire, and it will devour Bethel, with no one to quench it. Ah, you that turn justice to wormwood, and bring righteousness to the ground! The one who made the Pleiades and Orion, and turns deep darkness into the morning, and darkens the day into night, who calls for the waters of the sea, and pours them out on the surface of the earth, the LORD is his name, who makes destruction flash out against the strong, so that destruction comes upon the fortress.
—Amos 5:6–9

Welcome to this collection of short meditations for you who work for justice, stand in the breach, and lead sheep—some of whom don't want to be led!

The Rev. Dr. William Barber tells a story about how his "Grandmamma and her nieces always cooked for the whole family (and for anyone else who happened to stop by). …They also had a ritual whenever the food was done. Grandmamma would take a bottle of the anointing oil that she rubbed on people's heads when she prayed for them and slip it into the front of her apron. She and the other ladies would take some money, a rag, and some of the food they'd cooked and they would say, 'We'll be back shortly. We've got to go and hope somebody.'"[1]

Of course, Rev. Barber, who was a wise little boy at the time, thought she was misspeaking. He thought she meant to say she was going to *help* somebody, but he was wrong. Grandmamma

---

1. The Reverend Dr. William J. Barber II, *The Third Reconstruction: Moral Mondays, Fusion Politics, and the Rise of a New Justice Movement* (Boston: Beacon Press, 2016), 3.

knew what she was saying. She wanted to take some *hope* to people who, like herself and everyone she knew, were struggling to survive. Barber writes, "My grandmamma knew that any prayers worth their salt had to be accompanied by food for the hungry."[2]

We are instructed to *"seek the* LORD *and live."* It is a fact that if we *do not* seek God, we will flail in the waters of injustice and run out of strength. God needs for us to seek God so we will be able to go and "hope" somebody. The work you are doing is like standing in the kitchen and preparing food for your flock, people in your community who have been tossed and turned by corrupt and uncaring forces. The work you are doing demands the strength that only hope provides, because the empire is striving to fight back— fighting long, hard, and dirty—to shut you down.

It cannot happen. It cannot go down that way.

The one who made the Pleiades and Orion, and turns deep darkness into the morning, and darkens the day into night, who calls for the waters of the sea, and pours them out on the surface of the earth, the LORD *is his name, who makes destruction flash out against the strong, so that destruction comes upon the fortress.*

On this day, we pray, O God, that we remember the purpose for which You put us here. The arms of evil are too short to fight You; strengthen our arms so that we can sap evil of its strength. Stand with us as we affirm our faith in You and our determination to fight back against evil for the sake of *"the least of these"* (Matthew 25:40), who desperately need to know You are real. Help us to go out today and "hope" somebody.

---

2. Ibid.

Amen and amen.

DAY 2
GOD IS WITH US

Do not fear, for I am with you, do not be afraid, for I am your God;
I will strengthen you, I will help you, I will uphold you with my
victorious right hand.
—Isaiah 41:10

God is with us.

So many people I've met have been dismayed and angry over the political division in this county. The seeds of racism, hatred, and oppression are now yielding a pervasive and destructive crop. America has dealt with racist attitudes and policies before. White supremacist power structures have always promoted policies that were harmful to people of color, to women, and to the poor. Yet, in spite of their inability or their lack of desire to care for "the least of these," God has always been with us, equipping and empowering His faithful people to carry on in spite of oppression and hatred.

Beneath the shadow of injustice and intentional cruelty, we still wrestle with questions: "Where is God in all of this?" "Why must 'the least of these' continue to endure and endure?" It is not just African Americans who suffer. It is also the poor in South and Central America, Palestinians in their own homeland, and indigenous Americans, isolated on long-neglected reservations, as well as countless other impoverished and powerless people around the globe. It can seem as though God is no longer present. It can feel as though God doesn't care about the very people He told us to care for.

But know this: even when the oppressors seem to have the upper hand, it is the downtrodden and the oppressed who walk with God's protection and presence. Were it not for God, the masses would not, could not, survive. God has given us backbones strong enough to stand up under the pressure of poverty, cruelty, and inequality. Those who have never had to endure such inequity often find they do not have the strength to withstand it. I remember stories of white people who killed themselves during the stock market crash of 1929 and the ensuing Great Depression. Statistics tell us that the suicide rate in the United States increased from 17.0 per 100,000 people in 1929 to 21.3 in 1932. No doubt, black and brown people suffered even more, but over the centuries, they had grown strong spines to weather the pressure. Rather than seek the easy way out through death, they clung to life and tried to make the sun shine in a dark place. They knew how to do it because they had always had to do it.

God is with us. Should we wake up in the morning and find out that our candidate did not win an election or the ruling party once again attacked our civil rights, we need to know—beyond a doubt—that we will be all right, because we have always been all right. As the old hymn states, "Earth has no sorrow that heaven cannot heal," but it is also true that there is no evil, oppressive system that we cannot resist. We know how to do it because we have always had to do it.

In the book of Isaiah, the Lord says, through the prophet,

I will extend prosperity to her like a river, and the wealth of the nations like an overflowing stream; and you shall nurse and be carried on her arm, and dandled on her knees. As a mother comforts her child, so I will comfort you; you shall be comforted in Jerusalem. You shall see, and your heart shall rejoice; your bodies shall flourish like the grass; and it shall be known that the hand of the LORD is with his servants. (Isaiah 66:12–14)

There is no president greater than our God. Throughout history, oppressors have sought to weed us out, but they have not succeeded. The same people who, through their resistance, grew strong spines also have a lot of muscle. Those folks who knew how to make a pot of black-eyed peas last throughout the week, despite being forced to work to make their owners wealthy, are the same people who birthed us! We are progeny of people who knew this about God: *"He will feed his flock like a shepherd; he will gather the lambs in his arms, and carry them in his bosom"* (Isaiah 40:11).

Oppression damages those it targets. It weakens them but it cannot kill or eliminate those who hold on to God. It is simply impossible.

God is with us.

Amen and amen.

DAY 3
A PRAYER FOR OUR NATION AND HER LEADERS

I urge that supplications, prayers, intercessions, and thanksgivings be made for everyone, for kings and all who are in high positions, so that we may lead a quiet and peaceable life in all godliness and dignity.
—1 Timothy 2:1–2

God of us all,
      God of Christians and Jews and Muslims,

God of the people who believe in You and of the people who don't,

God of black, brown, yellow, red, and white people,

God of the rich and the poor,

It is to You, O God, to whom we pray this morning. We hold our hands out to You, lifting our hearts and asking You to incline Your ear toward us.

We need You.

We need Your guidance and Your presence.

We need Your voice and Your divine sight.

We know that nothing exists outside of You—even an election.

So we ask Your presence, Your Spirit, Your anointing, and Your divine presence for our leaders and our nation. On the Statue of Liberty are engraved these words: "Give me your tired, your poor, your huddled masses yearning to breathe free, the wretched refuse of your teeming shore."

The Christian Scriptures say, *"Come to me, all you that are weary and are carrying heavy burdens"* (Matthew 11:28).

A favorite hymn of the black church says, "Precious Lord, take my hand, lead me on, let me stand. I am tired, I am weak, and worn."

We are tired, God. We are weak and worn. We are huddled masses yearning to breathe free in a land that is supposed to guarantee our freedom. We pray that You would pick leaders who will lead us through this weariness to a new strength.

The people who belong to You say, "Amen and amen."

DAY 4
WHEN DARKNESS SEEMS IMPENETRABLE

By the tender mercy of our God, the dawn from on high will break upon us, to give light to those who sit in darkness and in the shadow of death, to guide our feet into the way of peace.
—Luke 1:78–79

The events that have taken place in our country over the last several years have taken the breath out of many of us. Our political process and civil oversight has been disturbingly partisan. A dark cloud hovers over everything, and it only grows darker and darker. The white, male power structure, which is determined to maintain its grasp of power, no matter the cost, seems intractable. This country's legacy of racism and sexism, written into the US Constitution, continues to rear its head at intervals throughout history, throwing people who work for justice into emotional and spiritual tailspins.

The fog of injustice appears to be impenetrable.

What happens in the dark? Growth. There are several plants that grow in the dark—including white asparagus, mushrooms, and potatoes. We've all seen it; the darkness cannot stop sprouts from appearing on the potatoes we store in dark pantries. I read that keeping potatoes in the dark slows down the process, *but cannot stop the growth.* Henry Miller wrote, "All growth is a leap in the dark, a spontaneous, unpremeditated act without benefit of experience."[3]

In our darkest hours, the "something" within us, which God put there, pushes back against the forces that try to bury our hope

---

3. Henry Miller, *The Wisdom of the Heart* (New York: New Directions Books, 2016).

and cause us to fall into a well of despair. The darkness of our lives claims its power and provides us with nutrients that only the darkness can provide. As a result, the threatening forces that come against us fail in their quest to destroy us.

The experience of being in the dark teaches us what we need to know and provides us with the elements needed for survival and success in fighting oppression. We learn things about ourselves we never knew before. Dr. James Cone said that those black people who have been oppressed, and continue to be, "must refuse to accept a view of reconciliation that pretends that slavery never existed, that we were not lynched and shot, and that we are not *presently* being cut to the core of our physical and mental endurance."[4]

The darkness over and around us is not meant to give us amnesia or to throw us into denial, two states of being that would make it easy to become complacent and apathetic. No, the darkness is meant to stimulate the parts of our being that we too often ignore, those parts of us that yearn to do whatever we must to *"let justice roll down like waters, and righteousness like an ever-flowing stream"* (Amos 5:24). It is in the darkness that our strength is made stronger, that our arguments become more pointed and vivid, and that our words become more inspiring, because only in the darkness can we "see" places that we cannot see when we are in the light.

The struggle for justice will never end; it has existed from the beginning of time. But the power we encounter when passing through darkness and struggle is something we must acknowledge and believe in. The song "Ain't Gonna Let Nobody Turn Me Around" is just one of what I call "songs from the darkness," songs that fuel our determination to hold on to God's hand and to fight the powers and principalities that want us to droop and die.

4. James H. Cone, *God of the Oppressed* (New York: Seabury Press, Inc., 1975), 208.

We shall do neither. Rather, we shall, like those plants that grow in the dark, begin to reveal our sprouts, produced by seeds the world didn't plant and cannot kill—sprouts that feed and grow in darkness before they emerge in the light.

Amen and amen.

DAY 5
TAKING SPIRITUAL INVENTORY

Do not be conformed to this world, but be transformed by the renewing of your minds, so that you may discern what is the will of God—what is good and acceptable and perfect.
—Romans 12:2

In her sermon, "Prophets for a New Day," the late Rev. Dr. Katie Geneva Cannon wrote that from time to time, we have to take a "spiritual inventory"—i.e., we must review what we are doing, and determine whether or not what we are doing is the will of God.

Taking such an inventory is a risk if we are truly serious, because, so often, what we are doing and what God wants us to do, what God sent us here to do, are diametrically opposed to each other. So many of us spend and waste valuable time trying to copy something or someone we admire, but when we do, we often find ourselves in spiritual turmoil. We were not sent here to sing someone else's song or write a story God has already assigned to someone else. Each of us has a unique purpose in this life.

We butt heads with God so often, and we blame God for the bruises that result from the fight. Maybe our resistance to taking spiritual inventory comes from a gnawing feeling in our soul forever reminding us that something is not quite right with what we are doing. We try to squelch that feeling, because, deep down, we suspect it is a sign that God's divine truth is trying to push its way through to our souls, where truth cannot be ignored.

What do we lose when we take inventory? We lose *the security of sameness.* In Dr. Cannon's sermon, she retold the story of the prophet of God and his encounter with King Jeroboam, who wanted to burn incense on the altar. This prophet had been sent by God to cry out against the sacrificial altars and idols of King Jeroboam. When the prophet carried out his divine assignment, Jeroboam became so angry that he reached out his arm to seize the prophet. But, Dr. Cannon writes, "in the twinkle of an eye, God caused the king's hand to become paralyzed." The king pleaded with the prophet to heal him, and, after the prophet prayed, the king's arm was restored. The king was now grateful and wanted to reward the prophet, inviting him to a meal, but the prophet refused, saying that he was "under divine orders not to eat or drink nor return by the same road on which he had arrived." (See 1 Kings 13:1–10.)

This nameless prophet had taken inventory; he was clear on what God wanted him to do. It must have been tempting for him, when he had suddenly gained the king's favor, to take advantage of the situation. We human beings like to be taken in and noticed by famous and rich people. But this prophet had his instructions, and he left the presence of Jeroboam.

There is more to the story Dr. Cannon shared, but what her sermon suggests, among other things, is that in this day and time, when so much of what we have always known in this country seems to have been compromised, overturned, or challenged, we might all need to take a spiritual inventory. What would God have us do *today*? What is God waiting for us to release, to let go of, so that, while we still have time, we can begin to live into our purpose? Who is it that we must let go of? What emotions and grudges must we release in order to be free enough to be a useful child of God?

The song "Hush! Somebody's Calling My Name" woke me this morning. I searched and searched for its history, to no avail; I did not find out when it was written or if it was sung by enslaved Africans. But after a while, I stopped. Being quiet, "hushing," as it were, is a part of the process of taking spiritual inventory. It is in the hushing that we hear God and are moved by God. If God is calling you right now, what is God saying? What are any of us refusing to hear or to accept? The psalmist writes in Psalm 62:5: *"Yes, my soul, find rest in God"* (NIV). In the taking of spiritual inventory, may we all find rest in God, and strength for the journey God set us on this earth to take.

Amen and amen.

DAY 6
BEING STILL

Be still, and know that I am God!
—Psalm 46:10

What is it to *"be still"*?

It came to me the other day that the psalmist was brilliant to put *"be still, and **know**"* before *"that I am God."* It is not enough to *"be still."* Being still requires that we know something about the goodness of God, no matter how much it seems otherwise.

It is in knowing God that we get our strength—strength to move and strength to *"be still."* African Americans in captivity had to "*be still*," even as they fought a most-heinous cruelty; only *knowing* that God would have the last word made them able to "*be still*" as they continued to work against the savagery of chattel slavery.

Being still is not an act of complacency; it is not stagnant. Being still is a verb, an action, which gives us the power to knock injustice off its game. The strength of those who *know* God is their ability to play offense, not defense, confusing and confounding an enemy that claims to *know* God, but in reality, only knows its own ideology, methods, and end goals.

When confronting evil, we cannot play defense. In knowing God, we are able to be still and yet play offense with the skill, grace, and power only the Master Coach can provide. Being still and knowing God does not mean we do not become impatient or, at times, even angry with God. God's working plan is so different than our own, all of the time. But God *is* the Master Coach. We have to *know* that. We have to first believe and then *know* that God's will is justice.

This recent season of political turmoil and uncertainty feels new to those who have not lived long enough to know that political evil is an ongoing evil; it ebbs and flows, but it never goes away. Our job is to "*be still*" yet do the work and seek shelter in our knowledge of the goodness of God. God *is* good—all the time—even when the game of life reeks with the stench of pain, evil, and injustice.

Knowing that fact will help us to "*be still*" and not give in to despair.

Amen and amen.

DAY 7

ADDRESSING THE BITTERNESS OF OUR SOULS

I am a woman deeply troubled; I have drunk neither wine nor strong drink, but I have been pouring out my soul before the LORD. Do not regard your servant as a worthless woman, for I have been speaking out of my great anxiety and vexation all this time.
—1 Samuel 1:15–16

One of the most poignant stories in the Bible is the story of Hannah, one of the wives of Elkanah, who, though loved by her husband, was burdened by her reality: she was unable to have children. Peninnah, Elkanah's other wife, took delight in Hannah's pain and often would *"provoke her severely, to irritate her"* (1 Samuel 1:6). Although Peninnah had sons and daughters and received meat at the time of sacrifice, Elkanah gave Hannah a *"double portion [of meat], because he loved her,"* and because *"the LORD had closed her womb"* (verse 5). He was puzzled because, in spite of his outpouring of love for her, she was not happy.

Her spirit had been damaged by the wind and driving rain that came with the trials of her life. We have all been there. Because of any number of experiences, our spirits either bend gracefully and dance with the forces that try to break us or they become rigid, because they cannot handle one more storm.

Hannah's spirit had become rigid. She was tired of hurting, tired of waiting, and tired of being mocked by Peninnah. Hannah *"was deeply distressed and prayed to the LORD, and wept bitterly"* (verse 10). God heard her and she soon became pregnant, but the bitterness of her soul had preceded her great joy.

It is only when we acknowledge that there is something ran-cid in our souls, caused by what we have experienced, that we can begin to live the way God intended for us to live. Bitterness within clogs us up. We cannot see or hear clearly. We pull away from God instead of drawing near. The bitterness we carry in our souls sep-arates us from the God we say we love, and we become estranged from the Source of our power and strength.

Bitterness, stuck in our souls, or perhaps planted there by our own hand, is a life-draining presence within us. We are filled with resentment and anger. We are children of bitterness, paralyzed by things that have already happened, or are happening now. We curtsy to bitterness, in effect, giving it a power it does not deserve, and we allow it to manipulate us to act in ways it wants us to act. But once we recognize and admit those things that cause us to be bitter, we can dismiss them; we have, in effect, conquered them and snatched away their power to drain us of life.

If we dare to face our bitterness, name it, and really give it to God, we are freed. That bitterness, which has drained life, hope, faith, and desire from us, becomes neutralized once we face it. Hannah faced the pain that had caused her much bitterness, and wept even as she prayed. There was no time to pretend that every-thing was all right, because it wasn't.

Her spirit was fractured, on the verge of shattering. She had come to the point where she could do nothing but create a hole in the membrane that covered her bitterness, so that the poisonous spiritual gasses could escape, freeing her. She didn't care what peo-ple would say to her or about her. She wanted this phase of her life to be corrected, healed, and changed. That's what she knew. She wanted to be freed from feeling bitterness when Peninnah taunt-ed her. She wanted a victory for her soul, and she knew only God could make that happen. Eli, the priest, thought she was drunk as he watched her lips moving, but she had already strengthened her spirit. She assured him that she was not drunk, but was, in fact, talking with God, getting rid of her *"great anxiety and vexation"* (verse 16). (See 1 Samuel 1:1–18.)

Addressing the bitterness in our souls is not pleasant, and it takes time, but to address it head-on is to give ourselves freedom. Bitterness within us begs to walk off with our spirits, claiming yet another victory, but the lesson of Hannah suggests that when we confront it, bitterness has nowhere to go but out of us, freeing us to live and to breathe and to relish the good in our lives, even as we acknowledge the things that have caused us pain, but will never rule our lives ever again.

Amen and amen.

DAY 8
THE GIFT GIVEN THROUGH SUFFERING

Who will separate us from the love of Christ? Will hardship, or distress, or persecution, or famine, or nakedness, or peril, or sword?
—Romans 8:35

There are times when the personal suffering endured by people is so immense, so deep, that it violates our limited capacity to comprehend. *Seeing* suffering does something to a person's soul—but only if the person who is suffering is seen as a human being.

When a person is not seen as a human being, he or she is not seen as capable of suffering. It has long bothered me that all of us hurt others at various times in our lives. For most of us, once we are aware that we have hurt someone or that we are causing another to suffer, we stop what we are doing. We feel a sense of shame or guilt. But when we see another person as an object, the dispensation of pain that causes suffering is not of importance to us. Through cognitive dissonance, we continue to inflict pain on others and think nothing of it; it is as though that person, or that group of people, is no more than bark on a tree. We lose our humanity, which includes the natural capacity to recognize and acknowledge suffering. When we treat others as inhuman, we become inhuman ourselves.

James Baldwin wrote, "People who cannot suffer can never grow up, can never discover who they are. That man who is forced each day to snatch his manhood, his identity, out of the fire of human cruelty that rages to destroy it knows, if he survives his effort, and even if he does not survive it, something about himself and human life that no school on earth—and, indeed, no church—can teach."[5]

What is this gift we receive through suffering? It is none other than faith—a faith not based on religion but on the persistence within our souls to survive. Those who have endured instances of personal suffering receive the gift, but those who, as a people or a group, have endured such suffering for generations have received this gift in an amount that even we do not and cannot understand. The spiritual strength, determination, and stamina of those who have endured and survived social suffering is like a precious metal or jewel, though, if the truth be told, we would rather not have had to receive either.

When we grow frustrated with God's apparent absence and/ or silence in the face of evil in our society, we sometimes turn away from God. It might be safe to say that by fighting against racism in this country, many of our strongest warriors turned to and away from God at the same time. While they knew it was only their faith in God

5. James Baldwin, *The Fire Next Time* (New York: Vintage Books, 1963, 1990), 99.

that would empower them to engage in their fight for justice, they were also confounded by what they perceived as an impotent form of Christianity, a religion practiced by whites that demanded respect of a God who apparently had no respect for them or their people.

People like Ida B. Wells-Barnett, Rosa Parks, Nannie Helen Burroughs, and others fiercely held on to God while simultaneously rejecting Christianity. In holding on to God, even though they could not understand how and why God would allow such suffering, they received the strength to stay on their course.

Because too many people have become inhuman, treating other groups of people as objects, social suffering will continue. Because of that fact, many more people will grow frustrated, angry, and confused by God, and even turn away. We might do well to remember that because of God with us, "Emmanuel," we have made it through some heinous experiences. We have "grown up," in Baldwin's words. We must pray that more people would lose their fear of turning toward God, and thus, develop *ears that hear and eyes that see* (Proverbs 20:12 NIV). But at the end of the day, we must thank God for the fact that, as the gospel song says, God has "kept me, so I wouldn't let go."

To God be the glory.

Amen and amen.

DAY 9
WHEN YOU CAN'T BREATHE

Thus says the Lord God to these bones: I will cause breath to enter you, and you shall live.
—Ezekiel 37:5

Every once in a while, I think of Eric Garner. He was the black man in New York who suffocated to death while being wrestled to the ground by police for selling loose cigarettes on the streets. On the disturbing video of the incident, you can hear him say, over and over, "I can't breathe!" I keep hearing his words, and I keep seeing the police ignoring him. It makes me shudder, but it also makes me acutely aware that even while we live, some of us are being wrestled to the ground by life and...and we cannot breathe.

The moment of the birth of a child represents the only time on earth that new life will be free from what life throws us. We have only a moment before the work of breathing begins.

The things that accost us, causing us to struggle, are many. For African Americans, racism has accosted us throughout history. Injustice in the form of sexism, poverty, poor education, and unjust justice systems—all of these and more cut off our breathing, causing us to struggle.

Life wrestles us to the ground and holds us there, like the officers who held Garner down. At times, there are those who observe, and, though they can do something to help, they do nothing. Most of the time, we wrestle with life on our own, with no witnesses.

I recently talked with a mother who had lost her son after a long, extended illness. He had been her light and her life, and now he was gone. Though grown, he was not old. His entire life was in front of him, and now he was gone. His mother sat in the lobby of the hospital even while his lifeless body still lay upstairs in his hospital bed. And now he was gone.

"I can't breathe," she said.

There are a lot of people walking but not breathing, not getting enough air in their spirits to give them life. They gasp from time to time, but there is no regular, rhythmic breathing. Their gasps snatch only enough air to give them the energy to keep moving a few more days, but not enough to jumpstart their spiritual lungs to work as they should.

There is a spiritual exercise which, if done consciously, is life-giving. First, take a "cleansing breath" to get the lungs ready for this intentional exercise. Next, *consciously* inhale the spirit of God and exhale all the elements of life that are accosting you, cutting off your capacity *and desire* to breathe. Consciously doing this takes our focus off the things that are accosting us and places it on the One who can free us. God, the present help in danger, shows up, because God wants us to breathe and live, in spite of life's hardballs.

A renewed and invigorated spiritual respiratory system gives us new life in spite of real life; it gives us the strength to push back against those things that are squeezing us, throwing us to the ground, handcuffing our capacity to fight back against injustice or pain or grief or economic despair, and, ultimately, suffocating us.

Only this very moment is promised; we have to strengthen our lungs in order to be strong enough to overcome the forces that are causing us to gasp. We are here to live and breathe in such a way that we can have life and have it more abundantly. This is God's desire for all of us, in spite of life "happening" to all of us.

Amen and amen.

DAY 10
TO WAKE UP AND WORK

Weeping may linger for the night, but joy comes with the morning.
—Psalm 30:5

Consider the words of Carlos Quijano, a Uruguayan lawyer, politician, essayist, and journalist, who said, "Sins against hope are the only sins beyond forgiveness and redemption."

Sin, we are taught, is anything that separates us from God, which means that hopelessness is a sin. God is hope, and hope resides in God. Without God, there is no hope. To reject God is to choose to rest and reside in hopelessness. When we give up, we are essentially saying that hope, which is God, is not real, and that situations and circumstances are greater than God.

Evil parades itself as all-powerful. In this political season, it *feels like* evil has won. Let's say, for a moment, that evil can and does achieve periodic victories. Even so, evil is not greater than God, and we who believe in God are called to walk in hope, to breathe in hope, and to trust in hope—which is to walk, breathe, and trust in God. We have the responsibility to do so.

In times of apparent hopelessness, we are called upon to seek "eyes that see" the hope, power, and presence of God. It is easy to "see" when evil rests, but far more difficult when evil rises up—and evil always rises up. Evil is in competition for our souls. Evil wants us to sink into despair. Evil wants us to sit in darkness and not believe in the light.

But if we have eyes that see, we are able to see how evil works. It comes to us regularly...but it also regularly passes on. Psalm 30:5 says, *"Weeping may linger for the night, but joy comes with the morning."* I always add, "...and morning *always* comes."

Nelson Mandela asked that our choices reflect our hopes and not our fears. He said, "Difficulties break some men but make others. No axe is sharp enough to cut the soul of a sinner who keeps on trying, one armed with the hope that he will rise even in the end."[6] Fannie Lou Hamer, an African American voting and women's rights activist, lived in hope; she believed that the evil of racism would be superseded by justice: "One day, I know the struggle will change. There's got to be a change—not only for Mississippi, not only for the people in the United States, but people all over the world."

We are called to hope. We are called to believe in what we cannot see, and believe that, even after we are gone, the work we have done will reap results. What we are *not* allowed to do is to weep and mourn to the point of inaction. Injustice and evil want to manipulate our spirits and steal our joy. Hope demands that we have "irrational joy," even as we trudge through the muddy terrain of injustice and hatred.

Sometimes it feels as though all of our hard-won lights are in danger of being extinguished. When we think of all the work we have done in the name of justice, and how much of it is in danger of being undone, our spirits are tempted to sink, but this thing called *hope* is our medicine. It is our spiritual castor oil, powerful enough to penetrate spirits that are clogged with despair.

It is now that we must sing louder and pray more fervently, even as we work...and even as we weep. This is not the time to doubt the power of hope. We must remember that weeping and evil and turmoil come, but they are temporary. They may bring the darkness of night into our lives, but the light of joy comes in the morning...and *morning always comes.*

Amen and amen.

---

6. From a letter Nelson Mandela wrote on Robben Island to his wife, Winnie Mandela, February 1, 1975.

DAY 11
LETTING GOD BE GOD

*Your iniquities have been barriers between you and your God, and
your sins have hidden his face from you so that he does not hear.*
—Isaiah 59:2

While many of the words in the Hebrew Bible are troubling,
some are more so. We are told that we are to love—*everyone.*
That is a strange command for people who have more of a desire
to "get even" or "strike back" than to respond with love and compassion toward those who hurt us or desire to hurt us. Jesus tells
us to love our enemies, and the writer of Romans says, *"Let love be
genuine; hate what is evil, hold fast to what is good; love one another
with mutual affection; outdo one another in showing honor. ...Beloved,
never avenge yourselves, but leave room for the wrath of God; for it is
written, 'Vengeance is mine; I will repay....' No, if your enemies are
hungry, feed them; if they are thirsty, give them something to drink;
for by doing this you will heap burning coals on their heads"* (Romans
12:9–10, 19–20).

In our humanity, we have little interest in being kind and com-
passionate toward those who have hurt us. In spite of what we are
told, we naturally desire vengeance. We take little comfort in believing that God loves our enemies as much as God loves us; instead, we delight in the thought that God might contribute to the
suffering of those who have hurt us by heaping coals on their heads.
We fear showing vulnerability or being perceived as being *weak.*
We believe that getting back at someone makes us look strong,
while forgiving them and loving them in spite of their cruelty is a
sure sign of weakness.

We must realize that the hate and retribution we wish on our enemies brings no peace to our lives! When we spend time and energy plotting how to get back at someone, we sin, because if sin is anything that creates *"barriers between* [us] *and* [our] *God,"* then our desire for vengeance supersedes the will of God in our life. When that happens, we cannot see God, and, frankly, we lose the desire to see God.

We cannot imagine how responding with compassion toward those who desire to hurt us will do us or anyone else any good. But in casting aside even the thought of treating an enemy with compassion, we lose an opportunity to see God work. God really can cut through the evil that rests and resides in our enemies. God can reach the part of a person's soul that no human is able to reach. God can convict even the most hate-filled person. When we take one step of compassion, God takes two steps by doing what only God can do.

We want the wicked to cease doing evil, and we want to help that process along. But we *cannot do what only God can do.* We are, in effect, asked a question that we are obliged to answer. God asks, "Child of Mine, do you think I can handle your pain?" We look at our pain and, in our hearts, we do not know. We have been told that God is all-powerful, but when dealing with our own pain, our own valley of dry bones, we do not know.

When Ezekiel faced his valley of dry bones, God asked the all-important question: *"Can these bones live?"* (Ezekiel 37:3) Ezekiel knew that to deny it was to doubt the restorative power of God. Ezekiel answered the only way he could: *"O Lord God, you know"* (verse 3). The moment we say that, God begins to work on our pain. We have room to give compassion, and we have room to let God be God.

Don't get me wrong. We still confront and resist evil when we see it done to us or to others. But our compassion for the people who have hurt us strengthens us for the journey; by doing so, we place burning coals on the heads of those who have hurt us, and the moment those coals are there, they begin to burn through whatever it was that caused that person to act as he or she did. Our compassion softens their hearts, as they cannot believe that we are resisting with nonviolence and that we are not seeking revenge.

Nobody ever said that walking with God is an easy journey, but doing so, if we take it seriously, will show us how strong we can be when we let God be God.

Amen and amen.

DAY 12
THE VALUE OF NIGHTTIME

You will not fear the terror of the night, or the arrow that flies by day.
—Psalm 91:5

In his sermon, "Bright Songs in Dark Nights," the late Rev. Dr. Gardner C. Taylor wrote, "You and I will never grow into what God wants us to be until we learn to pass through the nighttime." He continues, "When things go against us, when we are under stress, when we do not know how it is going to turn out, when it looks like it will not turn out right—you and I need that."

Many people in America are experiencing great stress as our country seems to be racing toward the edge of a cliff. So many of the gains made by oppressed groups of people—including African

Americans, immigrants, women, children, the elderly, and the poor—are being threatened or done away with completely.

America is experiencing nighttime, the likes of which many of us have never experienced before. For African Americans, nighttime is nothing new; we have lived through the night and learned how to survive and thrive with "night vision" a long time ago. But for those who have been used to living in daylight, and spared the *"terror of the night,"* seeing what this country is going through and where we might be heading is unbearable.

Dr. Taylor would say that this is a *good* time—a necessary and inevitable time. Nighttime always comes, no matter how long or bright our days may be. In the northernmost part of Alaska, residents do not see the sun for sixty-seven days in winter, but in summer, they have eighty full days of uninterrupted daylight. Neither the long night nor the long day last.

What do we do in our nighttime? Some retreat into the corner and allow the night to darken their very souls. Some bruise their souls and batter their faith by attempting to walk through the night on their own, *unattended and unaccompanied by God*. Others reach for God's hand and take it willingly and eagerly. In so doing, they receive the blessed assurance that they are not alone, that God hears, sees, and cares what they are going through. In doing so, they dissipate the terror of the night.

If America is in trouble, it is because we have given lip-service to our belief in God during the daylight, but now, in the darkness of night, we do not even know how to call on God. We have discovered that neither the gods of money nor earthly power can make the night easier to endure. America, though never perfect, is on a downward spiral and is too arrogant to call out for God to take her hand.

But for individuals who long ago learned to call on God in the middle of the night, to sing a song or pray a psalm, or to utter a prayer, even if it is just one word, we already know the value of nighttime. It is a place where we grow by default. It is a place where our eyes, straining to see through the darkness, become sharper, and where our spirits, connecting to the One who gives us the power and strength to make it to daylight, become more aligned with the Spirit of God. We know what these words mean: *"The Lord is my light and my salvation; whom shall I fear?"* (Psalm 27:1). We have lived through many a nighttime and we are still here.

Nighttime is a blessing. It is not pleasant, but it is better to endure the darkness with eyes wide open and hands outstretched, so that God can not only give comfort, but also lend us strength to make it through the nighttime and into the daylight that is *always* there. Our natural inclination is to sink into hopelessness and despair, but if we look for God and lean on God, we will receive divine whispers to remind us of the song that says, "Trouble don't last always."

It doesn't. Trouble feels like night, and night comes, but it passes. Sometimes more slowly than at other times, but it does pass. Gardner C. Taylor said God can give us "bright songs in dark nights."

Amen and amen.

DAY 13
THE PAIN OF BEING NAMELESS

You will not fear the terror of the night, or the arrow that flies by day.
—Psalm 91:5

One of the most painful components that result from being different is that your status as a viable and valuable human being drops a few notches. For any number of reasons, you are shunned and ignored, and people who you believed were your friends distance themselves from you so as to not tarnish, damage, or threaten their own positions in life.

In an essay entitled "A Strange Freedom," Howard Thurman called it a "strange freedom to be adrift in the world of men, to act with no accounting, to go nameless up and down the streets of other minds where no salutation greets and no sign is given to mark the place one calls one's own."

We descend into places of toxic isolation for a lot of reasons. In my own life, I found comfort and safety in staying by myself. I lived in foster care for a while and was then adopted by the man my mother married. I suddenly had a sister and a group of people who, I was told, were my "family," but I didn't know them. My mother chose to work as hard as she could to be accepted by this family—which, apparently, did not like her. They didn't like me, either; while she forged forward into the coliseum that hosts the fine game of making new relationships, I retreated into my own space, choosing isolation over relationship.

We do not understand the damage we do to ourselves until that self-imposed isolation finally reveals what it has done to our capacity to live a full life. In working to keep ourselves free, we have actually set ourselves up to face the most challenging trials we will encounter alone; in the time of our greatest need, we are ignored. We *feel* it in a way we have never felt it before. We realize that living in isolation has made us vulnerable to a type of pain we never knew existed.

But this kind of pain is not restricted to those who have isolated themselves; different groups of people—African American, Hispanic, the poor, women, ex-felons, Muslims—know this place as well. Both the isolated individual and the ones in groups find themselves living in this "strange freedom, going nameless up and down the streets of other minds ..."

It is being nameless that hurts so badly. Thurman says that it is our name that "marks the claim a man stakes against the world; it is the private banner under which he moves which is his right whatever else betides." Thurman continues:

> The name is a man's watermark above which the tides can never rise. It is the thing he holds that keeps him in the way when every light has failed and every marker has been destroyed. It is the rallying point around which a man gathers all that he means by himself. It is his announcement to life that he is present and accounted for in all his parts. To be made anonymous and to give to it the acquiescence of the heart is to live without life....

It is better to risk the breakup of relationships than to be so afraid of them that you refuse to try to build them in the first place. The poet Audre Lord wrote, "your silence will not protect you," and that is true; neither will placing yourself in isolation save you from being ostracized for any number of reasons. As risky as it may seem, it is better to be a consideration in the minds of some than to be nameless. In the same Thurman essay, the spiritualist wrote, "To be known, to be called by one's name, is to find one's place and hold it against all the hordes of hell. This is to know one's value, for one's self alone. It is to honor an act as one's very own, it is to live a life that is one's very own, it is to bow before an altar that is one's very own, it is to worship a God who is one's very own."

It is better, in other words, to connect with people so that they know us by name. For better or worse, those connections keep us away from the strange freedom that ultimately kills our souls whether in times of joy or of pain.

Amen and amen.

DAY 14

BECOMING A PEACEMAKER

Blessed are the peacemakers, for they will be called children of God.
—Matthew 5:9

One of the most profound lessons I learned long ago was the difference between a peace-lover and a peacemaker. Peace-lovers are those who avoid conflict, who "go along to get along," who believe that things will work out if they just don't cause trouble. Peace-lovers stand idly by while evil is doing its work. They see, but they will not act; they hear, but they will not listen. They cannot act because they refuse to admit that the evil before them is destructive. They don't want to get involved. During various periods of history, as well as present day, certain individuals and groups have remained silent while evil has been perpetrated on others. They are peace-lovers, wanting everything to just be okay without their input.

Peacemakers, on the other hand, understand that in order to have real peace, sometimes there must be confrontation. People who have fought for justice, who have stood in the lions' dens of the empire and risked life and limb, have been peacemakers. They understand, as Frederick Douglass said, that "power concedes nothing without a demand." They dare demand, and they dare stand their ground until someone hears their demand.

Many people think that to confront evil and injustice is to be out of the will of God, and yet, the story of God and of Jesus is one of continual confrontation with the powers that denied justice and fairness to all. We have both good (God) and evil (sinful systems of oppression) in our midst, and we, God's children, are called upon to confront evil as did Jesus Christ.

Mamie Till, along with all of the mothers and fathers of slain children whose deaths never received the justice they deserved, can rightly be called peacemakers. Her story is one that speaks to the awful burden of being a child of God, a peacemaker who refuses to back down, even in the presence of unconscionable pain. Ms. Till chose to look at the body of her mutilated son, Emmett, and refuse to be coerced by the people of Money, Mississippi, to quickly bury him, but instead chose an open casket funeral in Chicago so the whole world could see what had been done to her son. That is the act of a peacemaker. She was battered and bruised, her very soul was ripped to pieces, but she carried her pain into the palace of the empire and made them look at what they had done. She brought "peace," meaning she made the world confront the evil it perpetrated and forever altered the course of history in this nation.

Peacemakers understand that they will grow weary, but they do not let their fatigue drive the narrative of their lives. They understand that we are co-creators of justice and mercy with God, and that God depends on those who will walk into the lions' dens, no matter the risk of personal injury or loss.

Peace-lovers hide and in doing so, contribute to the perpetuation of evil and injustice for others and for themselves. Silence does not buy justice or ensure the peace that everyone says they want. Silence does not keep the same evil from being done to the next child.

To be a peacemaker is to radically stand in faith, be it Christian, Muslim, Jewish, Buddhist, Hindu, or any other brand. Peacemakers are often called troublemakers or rabble rousers, but the trouble and the rabble they kick up often result in baby steps of justice in a world that fights evil with every fiber of its being.

This is a perfect time to think about how to be a peacemaker in the presence of evil powers and systems that would love for us to remain peace-lovers. The powers that be can manipulate the spirits of people who are in need, with no thought of the people suffering by their actions. In the name of the God whom we claim as our divine Parent, now is the time to covenant to be a peacemaker, no matter the cost. Too much is at stake.

Amen and amen.

DAY 15
DEALING WITH DECEPTION

Do not lie to one another,
seeing that you have stripped off the old self with its practices.
—Colossians 3:9

No matter who we are, we all deal with deception. We deceive ourselves, we deceive others, and we are deceived by others. Along with deception comes betrayal, which also is three-fold: we betray ourselves, we betray others, and we are betrayed by others. It is a part of life, unfortunately, but how do we deal with it?

Sometimes deception is necessary. In nature, deception is often how an animal avoids being eaten by a predator. Likewise, there is always someone or something trying to devour us, trying to take our joy, quash our spirits, and destroy our confidence. And so, there are times when we must mimic nature's predators—putting on their confidence and displaying their command of their environment. Predators are dangerous but they are also instructive on how to survive. We can gain great confidence by imitating their antics and, in so doing, defeat them.

Necessary deception for survival can turn into self-deception if we lose sight of the fact that when a specific threat has passed, we must settle down and get in touch with *our true selves*. It can be so seductive to assume all the qualities of who people think we are and what they tell us, that we can internalize *their* ideas about us and stop working to explore the true depths of our own being. Anyone and everyone can have an opinion of us, but that opinion loses its power over us when we finally stop deceiving ourselves and decide to discover our true essence.

I once had a professor say that if you are accused of beating your wife and you are not sure if you have the capacity to beat your wife, you will get defensive, even if you didn't do it, but if you *know* that you would never beat your wife, you will not give an iota of power to what someone says you might do. It takes work to plow through all that we have internalized over the years, causing us to believe things about ourselves that are not true, things that keep us hiding behind a wall of shame, guilt, or insecurity. Doing the work, asking the hard questions, and accepting the answers that our spirits reveal helps to release us from the prison in which self-deception has placed us.

We are betrayed and we betray others.

We must go to God when we are betrayed and confess how we have betrayed others, praying for the healing of that person, even as we hurt from having been betrayed. Going to God in a moment of pain caused by betrayal so we might pray for those whom we have betrayed is an act of mercy required of all of us.

At the end of the day, there is no nirvana, no safe place where deception does not and cannot reside. We must learn to mimic those who have been through the fire and come out a little singed but still able to stand. We must learn to look to the hills from which comes our help to survive being betrayed, and look to God for enough ingestion of God's spirit not to betray others or ourselves. (See Psalm 121:1–3.) We must be sincere, for as Howard Thurman said, "Sincerity in human relations [with others and with ourselves] is equal to, and the same as, sincerity to God."[7]

Amen and amen.

DAY 16
DEALING WITH HUMILIATION

The one who is in you is greater than the one who is in the world.
—1 John 4:4

It has always struck me that in our country, it is okay for anyone who has been denied justice to be angry about it—except for black people. For some reason, our oppressors have made it nearly a mortal sin to be angry or to show that anger, while they feel no compunction or hesitation in showing their anger for things that seem much less provocative.

---

7. Howard Thurman, *A Strange Freedom* (Boston, MA: Beacon Press, 1998), 158–159.

Recently, I saw a white man ranting on CNN. Something had happened—I do not remember what—but I remember him saying something to the effect of, "I was marginalized. I felt marginalized! My rights were violated! Nobody likes to feel marginalized!"

Could I have really heard that correctly? Did he *admit* that *nobody* likes to feel marginalized? Contained within his statement was the reality that for many white people, people of color are not human. They cannot be called *anybody* or *nobody* because they—we—are not considered to be human.

His statement made me think about how we all must deal with the feeling of being humiliated. I recently heard a woman on the radio trying to explain to a man why she felt humiliated whenever men whistled or said lewd things to her as she walked down the street. She tried her best to explain how it made her feel, but the man did not and would not understand. "Aw, we're just having fun," he kept saying. "Yes, but it's not fun *for me*," she replied. He refused to "get it," and continued to defend this type of male behavior. To him, a woman was an object bereft of feelings and, therefore, it was impossible for her to feel marginalized and humiliated.

It also made me think how people of color are humiliated on a daily basis. A friend of mine told the story of how, as a medical student, he went into a grocery store and was stopped by a woman who assumed he was an employee. When he said he was not, she got angry and accused him of lying.

More recently, an African American veteran was at a restaurant on Veterans Day to take advantage of the free meal they were offering to vets on that day. A white veteran passed his table and said, "Back when I was in the army, we didn't let people like you fight." The white man proceeded to complain to the manager of the restaurant, suggesting that the African American was not really a veteran at all. The manager confronted the African American, demanding his credentials. After some back and forth, the manager took the African American's free food away.

Humiliation. There is only one way to handle humiliation, it seems, and that is with grace.

When feelings are a privilege reserved for a select few, the marginalized are not allowed to express anger at being humiliated. Ironically, it is the ones doing the humiliating who are devoid of feelings—well, certainly the capacity to feel empathy for anyone other than themselves. Therefore, any retaliation on the part of the humiliated and marginalized is fruitless. Nothing you do will cause the perpetrator of callous disregard to suddenly feel remorse for what he or she has said and done.

The only way to handle it is to hold your head up and open your spirit for a baptism of the Spirit of God, which gives strength. There will always be those watching to see how the humiliated handle their indignity. When we suffer humiliation and release our pain to God, those who oppress us are stymied.

At the end of the day, our connection to God—One who is greater than the forces around us—is what keeps us sane. It may not seem like a lot, but in a world where too many humans are willing and able to humiliate others, faith and grace are the only things that keep us standing and moving through the wilderness journey called life.

Amen and amen.

DAY 17
IT IS NO SECRET

Do not fear, for I am with you, do not be afraid, for I am your God;
I will strengthen you, I will help you, I will uphold you with my
victorious right hand.
—Isaiah 41:10

> It is no secret, what God can do
> What He's done for others, He'll do for you
> With arms wide open He'll pardon you,
> It is no secret, what God can do.[8]

We used to sing this hymn when I was a child. I don't hear it much anymore, but I found myself thinking about it when I learned something about hummingbirds. They are a miracle we can see. So little, they hover over plants extracting nectar, their wings flapping so fast they make a humming sound. Indeed, they beat their wings eighty times *per second* and have an average heartrate of 1,260 beats *per minute*. They move right and left, up and down, forward and backward, *even upside down*. They only use their feet for perching, not for walking or hopping.

It is no secret what God can do.

At this period of time in our culture and society, for some, the presence of God seems elusive.

Some cry out, "God, where are You?"

God would answer, "I am here."

---

8. Stuart Hamblen, "It Is No Secret (What God Can Do)," © 1950 by Hamblen Music Co.

But God might remind us what Jesus did when he rode into Jerusalem. He wept. While he was riding, he wept, saying, *"If you, even you, had only recognized on this day the things that make for peace! But now they are hidden from your eyes"* (Luke 19:42). He wept because the people, filled with "food" given to them by the empire, had been unable to fully experience God. Jesus saw that the people shouting, "Hosanna!" were in peril because they had not recognized *"the time of your visitation from God"* (verse 44).

When we lose ourselves in the realm of empire, we lose sight of God and the beauty of God's holiness. We become spiritually dysfunctional; our beings are so filled with the corruption and evil of empire that we can no longer inhale the presence and the power of God.

When that happens, we cannot see or appreciate the power of God. We cannot appreciate something as simple and beautiful as a hummingbird because we cannot inhale enough of God's Spirit that would allow us to do so.

Perhaps we need to engage in spiritual exhalation exercises, consciously taking in deep breaths and then expelling those things that are clogging our lungs and blocking our capacity to experience God. Perhaps we should consciously practice exhaling things like greed, anxiety, anger, envy, ambition—things that separate us from God—in order to make room for the Spirit of God, which gives us power and hope no matter our situation.

In the end, it really is no secret what God can do. If we have room, or if we make room for God in our empire-stuffed souls, we will be reminded that God...*IS*. We will be reminded that no matter how deep the darkness is, God, the Light, is always there. God will open our eyes to see the beauty of God's holiness—and to make us smile.

God will make room in our spirits to appreciate miracles like the hummingbird, which God has put all around us. Then we will whisper, "It is no secret, what God can do!" If God can enable the hummingbird to fly up and down, right to left, forward and backward, and upside down, then truly, it is no secret that God can and God will…because God already has.

Amen and amen.

DAY 18
"AND THEN I WAS SWEATING"

Even though I walk through the darkest valley,
I fear no evil; for you are with me.
—Psalm 23:4

God's Spirit within us is a treasure. It has kept people intact and in their right minds in the worst of circumstances. It has given those who wanted to give up the "one more breath" they needed to get to the next day, where they experienced deliverance, discovered answers, and found hope. God's Spirit within us is our power; it connects us with the living God, and equips us to get through, get over, or get out of dangerous places or situations.

I recently listened to a Greek Jew who survived the Holocaust. He and his family were arrested by the Nazis and sent to the Auschwitz death camp. He remembered when it seemed that the Germans were about to lose the war and the inhabitants of Auschwitz were told they were being taken to another camp. By this time, he weighed only 108 pounds. The snow and icy winds of winter made their discomfort all the greater. They had only the thinnest of clothing; no coats, gloves, or hats—and the trip was a long one. For miles they walked, day and night. Those who fell and were unable to keep going were shot on the spot.

The man wondered aloud, as he had done more than once during his time at Auschwitz, where God was. He struggled mightily but held on. God was all he had. But it was during this walk from one camp to another when he felt the power of God's Spirit. He thought about the weather in his native Athens. *It would be hot there*, he remembers thinking. He is not sure why his mind went there, but as he thought about Athens, something happened. "I was thinking about Athens, and then I was sweating."

He was beyond surprised. He had to put his hands on his face to make sure he was not hallucinating. He was not. God's Spirit within him had done something to make him sweat in sub-zero temperatures. He wept. He knew God was with him, *Immanuel*, refusing to let go because he had refused to let go of God. He made it to the next camp, where Americans soon arrived and liberated those who had been held captive.

The power of God's Spirit within is what fed and kept African Americans alive during slavery and the Jim Crow era. People of African descent ingested God's Spirit, and it kept them "so they wouldn't let go." They felt hope in the midst of what seemed a hopeless situation; in essence, they might have said "and then I was sweating," because they thought about freedom and justice, they thought about the next generation, who would need them to survive, and they thought about holding on to honor those who had not survived.

"And then I was sweating" needs to be the testimony of anyone who is in the darkest of valleys. We all have them, some more than others, but if we can imagine freedom, if we can imagine deliverance, and if we can imagine a new day even as the present day seems to be everlasting, we can experience the power of God's Spirit within us, welling up, and helping us to see our deliverance that seems so far away. God's Spirit within has brought many people through horrific times, and God's Spirit will continue to do that now.

"And then I was sweating." Let the redeemed of the Lord say so.

Amen and amen.

DAY 19
CLAIMING OUR PRIVILEGE

And God is able to provide you with every blessing in abundance, so that by always having enough of everything, you may share abundantly in every good work.
—2 Corinthians 9:8

We are used to talking about privilege, acknowledging that such a thing exists and working to get privileged people to recognize that they are, in fact, just that—privileged.

But dare I suggest that too many of us ignore the fact that we are *all* privileged on some level, even though many of us deny it just as vehemently as those whom we accuse of being privileged because of race and position of power. If there is such a thing as a "theology of sufficiency," are we missing the opportunity to take advantage of the things we have, while we whine about the things we don't have?

My work in Columbus, Ohio, involves working with the homeless and those facing extreme poverty. When I worked in the church, we would visit homeless shelters to give a meal to residents, but one day, a young man in line said, "Reverend Sue, this food is good, but we sure could use some good coffee!"

His words stopped me as I was scooping some greens onto his plate. I had never thought of including coffee on the menu because…well, because it was just *coffee*, and everybody can get coffee.

So when we began doing a different kind of ministry, we decided that we would go to those who are hurting and suffering, talking and sharing with them, and *offering them real coffee*. It was amazing to see how homeless people gravitated to us as we stood on a corner, handing out coffee that was too strong for me, certainly. They appreciated anything we had on hand to distribute, but to them, the coffee was a real gift.

Doing outdoor ministry requires you to be out in the elements, and in Ohio, those elements include ice storms, snow, and bitterly cold temperatures. Our first "coffee day" was around three years ago. When the day came, there was only one problem: it was what I call "stupid cold." The temperature that morning was about 10 degrees below zero.

I groaned because I hate cold weather and was mumbling to myself when one of the coffee crew called. It was about 6:00 a.m. "Reverend Sue," she asked, "are we going out today?"

Her question jostled me because even though it was cold, it never occurred to me that we should cancel the ministry. Within a couple of seconds, I replied to her, "Yep. We're going out. We have a choice to be out there but the homeless don't have a choice."

Her sigh was audible, and, really, we all looked pretty ridiculous out there, bundled like Eskimos in our parkas, hats, gloves, and boots. The homeless came scantily-clad—raggedy coats, porous gloves, if any, and very few hats. Most of them had spent the night in a shelter but had to leave by 9:00 a.m. because that's the rule. Some brought babies wrapped as well as could be but who were still gravely underdressed for the brutal weather.

It hit me that we who were giving out that coffee, bundled and protected against the cold, were privileged. I realized that I had spent far too much of my life bemoaning what I did not have—until that morning.

When I later attended the Samuel DeWitt Proctor Conference and heard about the theology of sufficiency (or TOS), I didn't make the connection between it and privilege, but slowly, the line between the two became clear. We are privileged, all of us, on some level. And just as privileged white people do themselves and society a disservice by not acknowledging their privilege, we all do God a disservice by not acknowledging *our* privilege. Once we begin to hone in on the fact that we are all blessed and highly favored, we begin to sprout new growth from our spirits, which comingle with God's own Spirit as we thank God for what we have and stop looking at what we do not have. We have all we need—and much of what we want. When we realize that, something happens within us. We experience an awakening that is a jump-start to a more fulfilling life, a life from which we give to others because we realize how much we have.

I thank God for that cold, brutal morning in Columbus, a morning when I, bundled up to protect against the bitter temperature, was allowed to see my own privilege. Nothing is as bad as we make it seem once we see what we have—materially, yes, but more important, spiritually. Sufficiency is a gift from God regardless of race or class or wealth.

Thanks be to God.

Amen and amen.

DAY 20
DO THE WORK

Commit your work to the LORD, and your plans will be established.
—Proverbs 16:3

N ot long ago, I decided I wanted to refinance my house. It seemed a good and a wise thing to do, but, lo and behold, there was so much *work* to do in getting the required documentation.

I do not like doing that kind of stuff. I don't like searching through files and boxes for mortgage documents and past bank statements. I just don't like doing all that work.

But if we do not work, we do not, and we cannot, "do life."

Howard Thurman, in a reflection entitled "Results Not Crucial," talked about how we must "do the work" if, and as, we pursue the kingdom of God.

In Luke 19, Jesus tells the story of a demanding nobleman who put a portion of his wealth in the hands of three servants before going on a trip *"to get royal power for himself"* (Luke 19:12). Before leaving, he summoned three servants and gave them each *"ten pounds,"* telling them to *"do business with these until I come back"* (verse 13).

You may be familiar with the story. Two of the three servants invested the money and earned a profit. But the third servant did not. Instead of investing the master's money, he feared disappointing the master he knew to be *"a harsh man"* (verse 21), so he hid the money for safe keeping. This third servant acted in fear, not in faith, and in his fear, says Thurman, he had "not done the work."

His actions angered his boss, not because he had not realized a profit, but because, he "had not done the work."

In this day of the megachurch, many preachers, pastors, and ministers get "caught up" in wanting all the flashy "results" of being a big church—attendance, financial giving, notoriety. Many people fighting for social justice also get caught up in wanting results— election wins, policy change, media coverage—and when they do not get the results they seek, too many of them simply give up and give in to disappointment.

Thurman said, "Results are not crucial. Much of the energy and effort, and many anxious hours are spent over the probable success or failure of our ventures. No man likes to fail. But it is important to remember that under certain circumstances *failure is its own success.*"

He went on to say that "to keep one's eye on results is to detract markedly from the business at hand. This is to be diverted from the task itself. It is to be only partially available to the demands at hand."

What are the "tasks at hand" in your life right now? What anxiety are you carrying because the results you desire have not come to fruition? And how has your work, your day-to-day work, been affected by your diverted attention from the work to the lack of results you are seeking?

This is a hard word, a hard thing to think about in a society that tabulates success by visible and measurable results. Going merely for "success" instead of being fully engaged in the work robs us, it seems, of moments of fulfillment that only *doing the work* can give. Doing the work is an act of love. We work to raise our children, we work in our gardens, we work to try a new recipe, not because we are sure of the outcome, but because our love compels us to work for someone or for something other than ourselves.

Thurman said, "The task of men who work for the kingdom of God is to work for the kingdom of God. The result beyond this demand is not in their hands. He who keeps his eye on results cannot give himself wholeheartedly to his task, however simple or complex that task may be."

The results are not in our hands. The work, however, is there, needing us to do it.

Amen and amen.

DAY 21

DOING WHAT MAKES YOU COME ALIVE

Commit your work to the LORD, and your plans will be established.
—Proverbs 16:3

Colin Kaepernick was an NFL quarterback who began "taking a knee" during the National Anthem before football games to protest the killing of young black men by the police. In an article about Kaepernick that appeared in GQ magazine, Christopher Petrella, a writer and scholar at Bates College, quoted the late Howard Thurman: "Don't ask what the world needs. Ask what makes you come alive."

The question struck a chord in me. Too many of us do not know what makes us come alive, and so, instead of thriving in life with the few days we have, we merely get by to survive. The song within us, uniquely ours and given to us by God, goes unsung.

I know a woman who was the head of a successful nonprofit organization. She took a principled but controversial stand on an issue that caused her board to discipline her. They wanted her to apologize for what she had said and done. She decided she could not do that and resigned.

There she was, talented, successful—and out of work. She applied to different jobs but received no interest. Then, one day, out of the blue, she said, "I have always wanted to be a butcher." I about choked on my coffee.

"Yeah," she said. "I've always been fascinated by how meat is cut and how butchers know how to give you exactly what you ask for. I'm going to see if I can do that."

Not long afterward, she landed a job as a butcher and quickly "moved up" in the field. Today, she proudly shows pictures of sides of cows or pigs that she has cut and her heart seems to burst with pride. She is doing what makes her come alive.

This woman was lucky that she had an inkling of what her "thing" was. Many of us do not. Or if we do know, we dare not think about it too much because we are afraid of the consequences.

Colin Kaepernick is out of work. He has been locked out of the NFL because he took a knee. He is vilified daily and criticized regularly. He may have lost the job he had, but he has picked up a new life. While he probably still feels the space in his spirit where playing football was front and center, today he also feels the space in his spirit that keeps him fighting against injustice and racism. Making bold statements makes him come alive. Working to help others makes him come alive.

If you are one of the few who knows what would make you come alive, you are blessed; many of us do not. What we *do* know is that we are not settled or at peace with where we currently are or what we are now doing.

When we decide to trust God enough and *do* what makes us come alive, we will experience the miraculous capacity and eagerness of God to make our hearts sing, even as we deal with what we must sacrifice. Doing what makes us come alive is a gift. We need to find it and do it, risks and potential losses notwithstanding.

God is there, always. And when we decide to sing the song our Creator has put inside of each of us, God will smile because we have trusted God in a way we never have before. My friend who is cutting meat has a smile on her face that is different than what it was. It's almost a grin. In fact, it *is* a grin, a divine grin given to her by God, who is comforted that this woman trusted enough to move into the space that God created just for her.

We all have such spaces. It is up to us to go to them and experience life abundantly before our days run out.

Amen and amen.

DAY 22
THE OIL OF STRUGGLE

How long must I bear pain in my soul, and have sorrow in my heart all day long? How long shall my enemy be exalted over me?
—Psalm 13:2

Many of us come from a theological environment that insists if we have faith, we do not have doubt. *Faith* and *doubt* are viewed as incompatible.

When I was a child, we had to take cod liver oil every day. Of course, we hated it, but my mother tried to make it better. She would pour us big glasses of orange juice—freshly squeezed by her, no doubt—then she would put a tablespoon of the foul-tasting oil into the orange juice and stir. No matter how long she stirred, the oil and the juice would not mix. The oil stubbornly floated on top of the juice and there it would be. We'd have to drink it, but in spite of the juice, we got the full effect of that nasty cod liver oil.

But faith and doubt *do* mix. Challenges, including bigotry and hatred, racism and sexism, homophobia, militarism, and so much more, are the oils we face each and every day. They do not *taste* good, but they serve a purpose: they strengthen us, just like the dreaded cod liver oil strengthened the immune systems of me and my four siblings. Every time we have to deal with injustice, every time we experience setback, personal or otherwise, we are forced to ingest an oil we do not like, and yet, those oils give us the determination to *push through*.

There is something about the oil of struggle that gives us stubborn resolve. We decide that the bad-tasting oils are *not* the bosses of us. We decide to not remain silent and pliant. And every time we do that, our spiritual natures grow stronger. Injustice has a function: to train us to fight. Even though the powers that be believe they can defeat us, they will discover, over and over, that those of us who have choked down the oil of struggle will not be stopped; we will not stay down. The oils only make us stronger.

We cannot have faith without having doubt. Doubt that comes from dealing with bad times is normal. We wonder how long we'll have to deal with what seems like an endless stream of evil. We want it to go away—but we have to understand that it will never go away. Faith means that we understand that no matter what comes our way, and no matter how hard, vicious, and ugly the battle, in the end, there is and will always be God. Faith doesn't mean that we believe we are supposed to see a victorious outcome of our battles; faith means that we believe in God to fight for us. Faith is more knowing about God's presence than it is knowing about how our fights will turn out.

In 1965, Rev. C. T. Vivian famously confronted Sheriff Jim Clark on the steps of the courthouse in Selma, Alabama, challenging him to stop keeping black people from registering to vote. On that day, Vivian did not know if he and all those who stood in the rain with him would get a victory. He was knocked down and arrested, but he didn't stop fighting. In the face of the bitter oil of racism he had been forced to swallow, his resolve only grew. Like the psalmist, he surely wondered, *"How long, O LORD? Will you forget me forever? How long will you hide your face from me?"* (Psalm 13:1). How long would the evil and hateful forces of racism prevail, with white religious people supporting it?

Oil and orange juice…doubt and faith…our lives are a testament to how we must always deal with both. They are always there. What we must remember is that as life spoons out those oils, we are getting stronger. We can hold on to our doubt, even as achieving God's will seems to be an elusive target. Doubt is not the opposite of faith; doubt is a part of faith. In fact, without doubt, there can be no faith.

Today, as we hear reports of evil triumphing over good yet again, remember that the oil of struggle exists along with the orange juice of the Spirit of God. Doubt is what we taste first, but the sweetness of the orange juice is still with us. As we cry, we rejoice. Doubt and faith, mixed together, will always reveal the glory of God.

Amen and amen.

DAY 23
PSALM 130

With the Lord there is steadfast love,
and with him is great power to redeem.
—Psalm 130:7

It is exasperating when we feel like we are crying out to God but God does not hear.

Psalm 130:1–2 says, *"Out of the depths I cry to you, O Lord. Lord, hear my voice! Let your ears be attentive to the voice of my supplications!"*

We all cry to God from time to time. But there are times when it feels as though we are talking to a deity who does not hear or seem to care.

In our current reality, it is exasperating that so many people seem to not hear the cries of oppressed people who have been in the storm for far too long. It is even more exasperating when people hear the cries but respond by spewing hatred and bigotry as the crowd cheers them on.

"Out of the depths I cry to you, O Lord. Lord, hear my voice!"

How can it be the case that there seems to be so little of God in God's people? How does that happen? And why can't, or won't, God fix it?

What makes a painful situation even worse are those who will not hear, those who continue to deny that racism still exists because slavery is happened so long ago. Recently, someone on Twitter posted a picture of one of the "beloveds" of African American history, Carter G. Woodson, along with a quote: "If the Negro in the ghetto must eternally be fed by the hand that pushes him into the ghetto, he will never become strong enough to get out of the ghetto." Then this person pushed her support for a racist political leader.

I was stunned.

It is one thing to vote for a racist political leader or favor their policies, but to quote the words of a civil rights icon, without any semblance of understanding of their context, in support of someone who blatantly stokes the fires of racial animus to rile up their base, is an unimaginable insult. The sting of the arrogance and ignorance is profound. It causes anger to boil up in the souls of black people, making some want to lash out, fight back, or set the record straight.

But human beings cannot set straight what spiritual evil has knocked out of alignment. Racism and bigotry are out of the will of God; our fight is against principalities and powers. (See Ephesians 6:12.) We are God's coworkers in a battle that seems as though it will never end.

"Out of the depths…"

Today, we cry out for a divine strength, a strength that will help us to channel our anger to motivate those who are moved to join us on the battlefield. To combat irrationality, ignorance, and idiocy, we must gather those who are rational, steadfast, and immovable. When we preach, people must see the same light we were given decades ago to lead us on our way out of the evils of racism. We *are* because God *is*. The people will put their trust in our light as they learn to ignite their own fiery torch.

> *I wait for the LORD, my soul waits, and in his word I hope;*
> *my soul waits for the LORD, more than those who watch for*
> *the morning, more than those who watch for the morning.*

(verses 5–6)

Our souls are waiting; our souls, dehydrated from having to walk through the heat of evil, cry out. We cry for hope and justice, gifts that fill our battered and weary spirits with the breath of God's presence.

We are marching "in the light of God," hatred and bigotry notwithstanding.

God of us all, hear our prayer and give us Your strength.

Amen and amen.

DAY 24
GOD IS SOVEREIGN, NOT INJUSTICE

Stand at the crossroads, and look, and ask for the ancient paths,
where the good way lies; and walk in it, and find rest for your souls.
But they said, "We will not walk in it."
—Jeremiah 6:16

This morning I arose troubled by thoughts of the injustice and hatred being promoted by lawmakers and politicians in this nation. And so much of it is done in the name of God, in the name of Jesus, and with the full-throated support of God's people. It's the same affliction that allowed "good Christians" to lynch people on a Saturday night and show up for church on Sunday morning ready to take communion so many years ago.

Just as in the days of the lynching tree, many of those who support injustice rely on the Bible as they do their work. God instructs us to walk in *"the ancient paths,"* the paths carved out by His Word and His will, but those who work for *injustice* also use verses like Jeremiah 6:16 (and others) to biblically justify their deeds.

The fact that people working for both racial *justice* and racial *injustice* are motivated by the same words of Scripture makes our work extremely difficult. Those who use God as justification to do evil have an arrogance that is supported by a false understanding of divine will. For instance, those who use Jeremiah 6:16 to justify racist behavior often leave off the last sentence of the passage: *"But they said, 'We will not walk in it.'"* In this passage, God is angry at those who ignore His Word and will, and He goes on to tell the Israelites what will happen to them because they continue to ignore His directives.

For those of us who work for justice, we must find encouragement in the fact that God is sovereign, not injustice. You are called, as the prophet Isaiah said, to comfort God's people. (See Isaiah 40:1.) You are called to tell them that *"every valley shall be raised up, every mountain and hill made low"* (Isaiah 40:4 NIV). You are called to remind people of the power of the glory of the Lord to be revealed.

> *You who bring good news to Jerusalem, lift up your voice with a shout, lift it up, do not be afraid; say to the towns of Judah, "Here is your God!"* (verse 9 NIV)

We have been taught there are not two Gods; our Sunday school lessons teach us that there is but one God, though those who work for injustice read sacred texts with an interpretation that is antithetical to what we've been taught. The smugness of those who use religion to do injustice can be unsettling and troubling, but you, workers who stand in the breach, "Shout!" The people of both the Hebrew Scriptures and the New Testament were just as prone to evil and injustice as are people today.

Shout! Lift up your voice; do not be afraid; say to the towns of Judah—to Baltimore, to Detroit, to Ferguson, to Oakland, to

Chicago—say to them, *"Here is your God!"* There is no evil—not racism, sexism, homophobia, nor militarism—that is greater than the power of God.

Say to them, "We are God's army. We will not be deterred. Not today. Not tomorrow. Not ever."

Amen and amen.

DAY 25
A COMMUNITY OF RESISTANCE IN SPITE OF

*Our struggle is not against enemies of blood and flesh, but against the rulers, against the authorities, against the cosmic powers of **this present darkness**, against the spiritual forces of evil in the heavenly places.*
—Ephesians 6:12

Archbishop Desmond Tutu wrote, "The Bible teaches quite unequivocally that people are created for fellowship, for togetherness, not for alienation, apartness, enmity, and division."[9] He cites Genesis 2:18, 11:1–9; Acts 17:26; Romans 12:3–5; 1 Corinthians 12:12–13; and Galatians 3:28.

Tutu refers to our beloved Bible and reminds us that it teaches us that all humans have worth because we are all created in the image of God. Apartheid, he said, "claims that what makes a person qualify for privilege and political power is that biological irrelevance, the color of a person's skin and his ethnic antecedents. Apartheid says those are what makes a person matter. That is clearly at variance with the teaching of the Bible and the teaching

9. Desmond Tutu, *God Is Not a Christian: And Other Provocations* (New York: HarperCollins, 2011), 158–159.

of our Lord and Savior Jesus Christ." Apartheid, he said, is "unjust and oppressive. ...positively unbiblical, unchristian, immoral and evil."[10]

Despite gains made in South Africa, the United States, and elsewhere, apartheid remains the unofficial law of the land, not just here but throughout the world. People of color everywhere are easy targets, separated first by the color of their skin and then by other things—gender, gender identity, wealth, education, religion, etc. Apartheid, which should be pronounced "apart-hate," exists as a philosophical construct all over the world, in spite of what the Bible says. Instead of working for a beloved community, the powers that be thrive and maintain their control by working to keep people apart, separated and hating each other. God's intentions are, quite frankly, ignored. God is pushed to the periphery of human affairs, forced there by the very people who say they love God.

Whether we want to admit it or not, we live in a nation that, for all practical purposes, still practices apartheid. The bearers of evil and division target anyone who is not them—people of color, of different religions, and of non-normative sexuality—and they do so with a vengeance. They firmly believe that a world divided is the only environment in which they can flourish and feel safe.

But what if believers in the God of all creation, presently mourning the ongoing oppression, took on a new boldness and a determination to, as Tutu says, show the "authenticity of religion."

Authentic religion allows us to mourn, to cry, and to bow under the weight of oppression, but it also mandates us to push back, armed with the truth of the power of the gospel and the knowledge that God is with us.

---

10. Desmond Tutu's "A Letter to Pretoria," http://kora.matrix.msu.edu/files/50/304/32-130-D29-84-al.sff.document.acoa000704.pdf (accessed June 7, 2019).

In the midst of our mourning, we must continue to be soldiers in the army. In the midst of this horrific pain, we cannot remain silent. We must be even bolder in our proclamation that Jesus is Lord, not politicians or CEOs or cable news pundits. Even in the darkest days of apartheid, Tutu would stand up to South African Prime Minister Botha, and all the other practitioners of that racist policy, and say, "You are not God!"

We are called to keep paying witness and to expose all the ways in which the rich and powerful treat people of color, immigrants, children, and other minorities, so that the light will shine in this most present darkness.

God will hear us. God *hears us now*. Psalm 46 reminds us: *"There is a river whose streams make glad the city of God, the holy place where where the Most High dwells. God is within her, she will not fall; God will help her at break of day. Nations are in an uproar, kingdoms fall; he lifts his voice, and the earth melts"* (verses 4–6 NIV).

We mourn the existence of corruption and racism at the high levels in our country, but we must rejoice at the same time and declare the immorality of hatred. God is within *us*. And God will help us at break of day

Amen and amen.

DAY 26
COMMITTING TO GOD

Jesus called out with a loud voice, "Father, into your hands I commit my spirit." When he had said this, he breathed his last.
—Luke 23:46 NIV

Life does not lend itself to committing to God. Instead, it throws us too many curveballs. Life does not care who we are, how popular or well-known we are, what we stand to lose, or how we feel about anything that happens to us. Life just plows forward, telling us, in essence, "Deal with it."

Dealing with life is difficult. We do not understand why what happens, happens.

The existence of evil has troubled people for generations. If God is our ever-present source of hope, why do we experience hard times? It seems that a God who desires community would stand in front of Her people, protecting them from the evil that strives to annihilate them. But God does not do that, any more than God stopped Jesus from succumbing to death on the cross.

It seems that the only and best thing to do when evil forces have us by the heels is to say the exact words that Jesus said when death was upon Him: *Into your hands I commit my spirit.* There is a certain release and relief that comes when we say those words, when we acknowledge that though this present moment is troubling, frightening, or even unfair, we believe that God is greater than all of it. God, the Lover of all souls, the Creator of all human beings, and "the Force" that battles evil all around us, ultimately will have dominion over this thing that is causing our turmoil—even if it kills us.

Years ago, I ministered to a young girl who had bone cancer. She was in horrific pain. The "church people" had come to visit her, to pray over her, and to apply oil to her forehead, all in hopes of bringing more of God into her thinking and praying. She called me late one evening, crying. "I already have faith!" she kept sputtering. "I have faith, but they don't believe me!"

A day or two later she was in the hospital. Cancer had invaded every part of her body. A tumor was growing out of her eye. The weight of a sheet on her ravaged body caused her to cry out. Pain medication only granted her a short break from her agony. On most days when visiting her, you could hear her moans from the moment you got off the elevator.

Not this day, however. When I got to her room, she was smiling. I thought she must have been heavily medicated, but her nurse said, "I don't know what's going on. She's been quiet and smiling all morning. We haven't done anything different."

As I drew near, she whispered, "I told you I had faith, Reverend Sue. Jesus heard me. Jesus knows. I told Jesus I committed myself to Him. I said those words, *'Into your hands I commit my spirit.'* And God gave me peace."

I was stunned. Yes, we had talked about those words, plenty of times, but I had never *seen* the words come to life. I'd never seen them literally speak life into a tormented being. She was still in pain, she said, but she knew God was with her. She knew that God had not abandoned her. Let's call that "the Force." "The Force" came to this young, vibrant woman, and took the power of the evil away. Evil had been supplanted by the power of "the Force," God, in that child's body and, more importantly, in her spirit.

She died two days later, at home. When I visited her on the morning she died, I was stunned yet again. She was smiling. She died that way…smiling. Her mother said that not long before she passed, she grew quiet and smiled. She heard her daughter say, *"Into your hands…."*

When we surrender and trust God like that, even in our darkest moments, God, "the Force" does what only God can do. That commitment to God, the commitment of our spirit, placing our spirits into the very hands of God, removes evil from our space and lets God be God, as only God can.

There is no greater gift God can give us.

Amen and amen.

DAY 27
LEARNING WHO YOU ARE

Those who wait for the LORD shall renew their strength, they shall mount up with wings like eagles, they shall run and not be weary, they shall walk and not faint.
—Isaiah 40:31

One of the most powerful stories I have ever heard is that of a little eaglet who found himself mixed up in a family of baby chickens and so began thinking he was a chicken too. Only he didn't look like the other members of his new family. While the baby chicks were cute and fuzzy, the eaglet looked scrawny and bedraggled, with very few feathers on his body. Neither the other chicks, the mama chicken, nor the humans who passed by paid this eaglet much attention.

He began to internalize a feeling of inferiority.

One day, a visitor came to buy some grain from the farm where the eaglet lived. He looked into the pen and noticed that a baby eaglet was mixed in with the baby chickens. The farmer refused to believe that the ugly chicken was an eagle but the man persisted. Finally, the famer gave in. "Fine!" he bellowed. "If you think you know so much, take that ugly bird with you at no charge and get

out of here. I'll let *you* raise it and find out how little it is worth."
Of course, the baby eaglet heard all of this and was sad. The visitor
picked up the eaglet and held it close to his chest, mumbling, "One
day, you will know who you are."

He took the bird home and put him in the pen with the other
baby chicks and let him be.

The eaglet grew and before long, it was clear even to him that he
didn't look like the other chickens. They were kind of dumpy. They had
little tiny feet and feathers that seemed to be all over the place. Some
were brown, some were white, but all of them looked and sounded
like each other. He, on the other hand, was tall and sleek. His feathers
were a deep chestnut brown, except on his head and neck. There the
feathers were the whitest white ever. His beak was long and yellow.
While his brother and sister chicks seemed to have a hard time even
seeing the grain on the ground in front of them, the eagle noticed that
he could see far away, even while standing on the ground.

Still, he did not know who he was or what he was. He was very
sad.

One day, his new owner took him to a high hill overlooking
a canyon and told him that he was an eagle that was meant to fly.
The eaglet, who was still very young, shook. With no further in-
struction, the man threw the eaglet into the air. As he began to
fall, the eaglet cried out, "Help! Save me!" The man ran down the
hill and caught the eaglet. He climbed up the hill and threw the
bird into the air again, but the same thing happened. As the man
prepared for a third attempt at flight, he said, "You are an eagle.
You were meant to fly. This time, I will not run to catch you. You
are an eagle. You can do what you were made to do." As the eaglet
was tossed into the air again, he looked back and saw that the man
was not running to catch him. As he started descending, he heard

the man's voice, "Arch your back!" The eaglet didn't know what that meant but as he descended, something inside of him took over and he arched his back. His wings left his sides and seemed to stretch out forever. In amazement, he began to move them. It was only then that he realized…*he was flying!*

God had made the eaglet to fly but he had been sitting in painful insecurity, comparing himself to chickens, none of whom would ever be able to do what he was doing now.

He looked back for the man but he was gone. The eaglet soared and soared and, finally, after so many days of feeling sad and unwanted, began to ascend into his destiny.

God watches us as we are unaware of who we are. God sees us comparing ourselves to others and finding ourselves lacking. God sees us holding back from doing what God has gifted us to do. In comparing ourselves to others, we have abandoned becoming the person God created us to be.

On this day, God is standing on a high hill, throwing us out there one more time, beseeching us to trust in who we are. God already knows; God only wants *us* to know.

God calls out, "Arch your back!"

If we are frightened enough, we will stop comparing ourselves to others and that divine "something" within us that God put there will take over and begin to do the work for us. The gift deep inside your identity will reveal itself and you will do what you were created to do. You will arch your back, stretch out your massive wings, and begin to soar.

And God will smile.

Amen and amen!

DAY 28
LOVING GOD ENOUGH TO LOVE OURSELVES

*Little children, you are from God, and have conquered [the evil
spirits of the world]; for the one who is in you is greater than the
one who is in the world.*
—1 John 4:4

We are so obsessed by the world in which we were raised. The
perceptions we hold of ourselves are so intermingled with the
words and opinions of those who raised us. We ingest their words,
their ideas, and their concepts of right and wrong. Some of those
things are helpful, but in all honesty, much of it is not.

I heard a story about two Latinx girls who grew up in Texas in
the 1950s. Of course, the schools were segregated and all Latinx
children went to a certain elementary school. Many of the children
spoke only Spanish; others spoke English, but only as a second
language.

One day, a first-grade teacher told her students to take out a
piece of paper and write down, "I will not speak Spanish in school."
The students did as they were told. Then they returned their newly
written declarations to their teacher. All of the other teachers in
the school, it seems, were having their classes do the same exercise.
In each classroom, the teachers had cigar boxes into which they put
the declarations. Then all of the students were marched out to the
flagpole in front of the school.

As they gathered at the flagpole, they noticed a hole. The
teachers placed the boxes with the students' declarations into that

hole and covered them with dirt. As one of the teachers put it, it was the day they "buried Mr. Spanish."

The now grown woman telling the story remembered how insulted she felt. She was only six years old at the time but she had been to funerals. She understood the implication of what had just happened. Incensed, she turned to her group of friends and, in Spanish, said, "I will never stop speaking Spanish!"

Unfortunately, a teacher heard her and paddled her so harshly that she had bruises on her body. She went home, crying and angry, and stayed there for three days.

Her father was upset at what had happened but advised his daughter to comply with her teacher's instructions. He didn't confront the school about what its teachers had done and he didn't challenge them over the excessive discipline that had brutalized his daughter.

The story was heartbreaking on a number of levels, but it made me think of how we, living in an oppressive society, often end up giving more power to the empire and its policies and practices than we do to God. Too often, we give in and offer our children bad advice—either through our words or our actions. Those children grow up with warped opinions about themselves; they become followers rather than leaders, not trusting God enough to stare injustice in the face and dare it to continue its deadly ways.

When we love God, not just with our lips but with our lives, something happens inside us. We feel the presence of God. We experience the nudging of God in the face of evil, wrong, and injustice. We find that we cannot remain compliant, silent, or inactive. When confronted with injustice, we are called to act and to *show the world* who God is. We must refuse to accept it when the empire puts people down and shuts them out—especially our children.

Deep down in our very souls, we want our children to know who they are and Whose they are. They know this, in part, from watching us when we march into the lion's den. When we do that, we show that we love and understand who God has made us to be, and we are willing to "go to the mat" for that same God. We lose our fear; we lose our shame and timidity; we walk boldly into the fire in order to show that God is sovereign, not the empire and its cronies.

The woman telling the story of having to "bury Mr. Spanish" remembers that day as vividly as though it happened yesterday. She said little about her father and his advice to her, but she has held on to her conviction that she, as a Latinx, had rights. And one of her rights was to speak the language of her heritage. She has taught her children the same.

At the end of the day, maybe it's loving God enough to love ourselves that will ultimately put the empire in its place, taking away its arrogant assumption that it is greater than our God.

It is not, plain and simple.

Amen and amen.

DAY 29
THE FINE ART OF SELF-FORGIVENESS

If anyone is in Christ, there is a new creation: everything old has passed away; see, everything has become new!
—2 Corinthians 5:17

It is one thing to forgive another person for a wrong done to you but it is quite another to forgive yourself for all the wrongs we humans do.

A person who lives in his or her guilt is a tormented soul. The memory of the offense haunts and follows that person and sticks to his or her spirit like a shadow. There is no escaping it. The guilt and shame often lies dormant, like a dormant cluster of cancer cells, but intermittently, the guilt—that cancerous soul infection—awakens and reminds us of all the damning things we'd rather forget.

It does not matter that God has already forgiven us. Even if we know that, we probably harbor doubts about whether it is true. After all, if we truly believed that God totally forgave us, we might be able to forgive ourselves. But we don't. No, we continue to wrestle with our flaws and mistakes. No one can beat us up like we can beat ourselves up.

We all have skeletons in our closets. Some are better able to ignore them but their false bravado is just a method of covering up their guilt and shame.

I once had a conversation with a man who, when he was young, dropped out of contact with a woman to whom he had been engaged. "I just didn't want to marry her and I didn't have the courage to tell her," he said. "I changed my phone number. I got another job and moved out of state. I never told her a thing. I kept her believing that we were getting married until, one day, I was just gone. I never spoke to her again."

His story was troubling on a number of levels. As we talked through it, I asked him, "What bothers you most about what happened?"

"I can't forgive myself for being such a coward," he said. "I don't know what I expected her to do if I had told her I didn't want to get married. I was just too chicken to tell her the truth."

The incident had happened many years prior to our conversation. Even though he had since found her and apologized, and though she seemed to have accepted his apology, he still could not believe that her forgiveness was genuine. Nor did he believe that God had forgiven him. He definitely could not forgive himself.

"If I had been dropped like that," he said, "I would *never* forgive the woman who had done that to me."

This man ended up in therapy, but not even therapy could get him to forgive himself. "I caused her a lot of pain," he said. "I can never change that."

None of us have the power to change the things we have done or said in our past that have caused others pain. But if we do not forgive ourselves, we restrict our capacity to grow. God uses our flaws, shortcomings, and mistakes to make us stronger. If we do not allow ourselves to come face to face with our flaws and then give them to God, we rob ourselves of the opportunity to experience new life in spite of all those things we wish we could forget. Allowing God *in* is the art of self-forgiveness. God kneads our lives, working all of our flaws in with our strengths to make us whole. Our past weaknesses and mistakes are what give our life power, and God gives us the boldness to risk forgiving ourselves so that we can walk in newness.

This man never married, even though he wanted to. He continued to punish himself, even though God had moved on. He let his mistake define his life instead of allowing his mistake to season and strengthen his life.

There is an art to letting God into our troubled and shackled souls, but if and when we do, God allows us to see our flaws and our past as part of what has made us who we are today. Self-forgiveness becomes the embodiment of the Scripture, *"If anyone is in Christ, there is a new creation: everything old has passed away; see, everything has become new!"*

Even our past.

Amen and amen.

DAY 30
THE HOLES THAT WON'T HEAL

We are afflicted in every way, but not crushed; perplexed, but not driven to despair; persecuted, but not forsaken; struck down, but not destroyed; always carrying in the body the death of Jesus, so that the life of Jesus may also be made visible in our bodies.
—2 Corinthians 4:8–10

Part of the reason there is so much pain in our current political climate is due to the viciousness of the dialogue. The name-calling, the put-downs, and the humiliation and denigration of so many people has no precedent in recent history. We erroneously believed that people would hear the vile words and threats of a presidential candidate and that they would be repulsed and vote against him. And even though the majority of voters did just that, far more people than expected—Christian people—ignored his words and voted for him anyway.

The fact that *so many millions of people* resonated with those words puzzled people.

Our country is divided. There are those who deplored the way racist candidates spoke and acted; there are those who *pretended* to deplore it but voted for him anyway; and there are those who completely resonated with the hate and vitriol. These people seem to not care or even rejoice by how the president's words cut at the very fiber of people of color who lived with and under oppression for so long. They seemed to care little that black children were being called the "n-word," that Latino and Latina children were being taunted and warned that they would be deported. They seemed unaware and unconcerned that many women were feeling marginalized and dehumanized, and that Muslim-Americans were walking in fear, not sure of who would attack them and get away with it.

Howard Thurman wrote of a time when, as a child growing up in segregated Daytona Beach, Florida, a white boy attacked and jabbed him with a pin as he mowed the lawn of a white person. As Thurman gathered his wits and struggled to deal with the pain, the white boy said, "Ha! That didn't hurt you! You can't feel!"

The audacity of the arrogance of oppression is hard to accept and yet, that arrogance accompanies oppressed people, as it always has. The dehumanization of God's children who happen not to be white has been far-reaching and deeply ingrained. All oppressed people have to reach for God in order to stay above the waters of anger and despair.

As more election cycles loom in our future, the caregivers are wrestling with their own emotions—anger, bitterness, sadness, etc.—even as they try to comfort the disheartened who are looking for God in this space, thick with the racial, sexual, cultural, and religious fog of oppression. Many faithful believers are struggling for breath; indeed, they are being choked by the pressure of oppression, and are in no less danger of dying than was Eric Garner, who, as a police officer wrestled him to the ground, cried out, "I can't breathe!"

The little boy who jabbed Howard Thurman was wrong. *"That didn't hurt you! You can't feel!"* Yes, people of color feel; and yes, it does hurt; and yes, it's been hurting for a long, long time. The hateful words of racism and white supremacy leave holes in our spirits, but this has been going on for generations. We are in a constant state of regeneration and healing.

There is a story of a little boy who was once walking past a fence with his grandfather. The grandfather gave the boy some nails and a hammer and told him to hammer the nails into the fence post. The boy was puzzled, but he did it. The next day, as they walked by the same fence, the old man told the boy to pull out all the nails he had nailed into the fence the day before. Puzzled again, the boy did as he was told.

When all the nails were out, the grandfather asked the little boy, "What do you see?"

The little boy said, "The pretty fence is all ruined. There are holes in it where the nails used to be."

The grandfather shook his head slowly and said, "That's what happens when people are not good to each other, when they say unkind things to each other. They leave holes in each other and they are never the same. The holes do not go away."

Oppressed people know that pain in a way that the oppressor does not because he cannot.

The only reassurance we have is that God…*is.* Paul reminds us that we are *"afflicted in every way, but not crushed; perplexed, but not driven to despair; persecuted, but not forsaken; struck down, but not destroyed."*

The holes caused by oppression are the permanent scars we carry; they are now a part of our DNA. But so is the grace and the presence of God. In the end, it is the latter that "trumps" the damage done by those who would annihilate us.

Amen and amen.

DAY 31
WHEN OUR BACKS ARE BENT

Since we are surrounded by so great a cloud of witnesses, let us also lay aside every weight and the sin that clings so closely, and let us run with perseverance the race that is set before us, looking to Jesus the pioneer and perfecter of our faith.
—Hebrews 12:1–2

I recently watched the movie *Queen of Katwe*,[11] which tells the story of Phiona Mutesi, who escaped a life of poverty in the Katwe district of Kampala, Uganda, after she learned to play chess. Before this, her life had been defined for her and she had resigned herself to live in it. This was a girl who knew pain, suffering, and lack. Her father died of AIDS when she was three years old. She also had an older sister who died of unknown causes. When she was nine years old, she dropped out of school because her mother could not afford to send her anymore. She and her siblings sold maize on the streets of Katwe. But in time, she discovered a program run by a Christian sports mission. There, she met Robert Katende, who taught soccer and other sports to area children.

He also taught chess.

---

11. *Queen of Katwe*, directed by Mira Nair (2016; Walt Disney Studios).

Phiona was taken with the game. Though she could not read, she had a brilliant mind and began to excel at it, exceeding expectations and beating the most formidable opponents, including boys who did not believe girls should be able to beat them.

There were two lines in the movie that struck me. One was: "In this game, what is little can become big." The other was: "Sometimes, where you have been is not where you belong."

It struck me that many of us are in the places where we have always been, believing it is where we belong. We have bought into the opinions of family, friends, teachers, and society. They have given us their evaluations of who we are, what we can do, and where we are supposed to be. They have labeled us and put us in a cubbyhole, where we have stayed put. But too often, where we *are* is not where we *belong*.

When things got difficult for Phiona in chess competitions, she grew frustrated and looked back to the life she knew before. Things were certainly difficult in her village, but she knew the drill. But this new rejection and pain she endured as she moved into a new sphere was scary—and she did not like it. It was Robert Katende, her coach, who gently taught her that moving to the place where we belong is fraught with difficulty, but worth it in the end. Gradually, as Phiona Mutesi learned to master chess, she found herself moving further and further away from the life she had known.

In moving from a place of comfort into a wider world, "little" Phiona became "big." She discovered the immense brilliance God had given her. Not only did she grow into the place God had for her, but she was able to help her family as well. Being willing to *go*, as opposed to *staying* where we have always been, puts us in a place where we can help others as well.

There was one other line of dialogue from this movie that struck me. Phiona was in the midst of a difficult chess match, playing for a championship. She was nervous and making poor moves because she was beginning to doubt that this was where she belonged. In the movie, her coach broke protocol and hollered, "You belong here!

The sound of his voice jostled her spirit. She looked at him, and at those who had come to support her, and she was able to receive spiritual feeding. Yes, she did belong. When she internalized it, her spiritual spine was strengthened and straightened, and she was able to play *her* game. She won the match and never looked back after that.

When we walk with bent backs, carrying rejection, self-denigration, and self-doubt, we cannot see what is waiting in front of us. God wants us to stop struggling with the burdens that keep us from going to where we belong. God wants us to understand that in this experience called life, what is *small* can become *big*, and that, whatever we have been told in the past, *we belong* in this place where God has led us.

With our spines straightened, we can do all things. That is what we must always remember.

Amen and amen.

DAY 32
WALKING ACROSS ROPE BRIDGES

Jesus looked at them and said, "With man this is impossible, but with God all things are possible."
—Matthew 19:26 NIV

It has occurred to me that if we find ourselves in a place we do not want to be, very often, it is our own doing.

Too often, we decide who we are based on what our parents or friends or teachers or people we love and respect tell us. We ingest their opinions, their biases, even their fears and their issues. We buy into what they say we are; in effect, we build boxes for ourselves according to their specifications and blueprints. Even if we are uncomfortable in those boxes, we remain in them, wasting valuable days and hours.

I will never forget taking a group of people to West Africa. One of our delights on that trip was going to Kakum National Park, where there are seven rope bridges hung from the jungle canopy, 131 feet above the floor of the rainforest. We were excited to get to the bridges but when we finally arrived and saw how narrow and unstable they appeared, some in the group audibly gasped. To be honest, I did not want to walk across that first bridge, let alone seven of them! But the group was looking to me. I had brought them there. The unspoken question hung in the dense jungle air: "What are *you* going to do?"

I took a deep breath. My son, who was about eleven years old at the time, said, "Come on, Ma!" And he started across. I gasped even looking at him. I wanted to shout to him to be careful but I stopped myself. The bridges had been there a long time; many people had walked across them. He was safe—and I would be too.

I took a deep breath and began to walk across the bridge, afraid to look down. Of course, my son called out, "Look down, Ma!" It was breathtaking and scary, but more breathtaking than scary. The beauty of God's holiness was right there and I was being allowed to see it.

I did all seven bridges and was quite proud of myself as I returned to the starting point where others in the group were still waiting to go across. I encouraged them: "I'm still alive! Go on!"

Scared and tentative, one by one, they got in line. They were moving along, when suddenly, one person in the group turned around halfway across the first bridge and came back. Tears were rolling down her face. "I'm scared," she said. "I can't do it." I was stumped. She had made it to the middle of the bridge. All she had to do was keep going, but she came back.

She had put herself into a box that was too small. She did not, and could not, allow herself to break out of that box and take the steps that would lead her to where God wanted her to be.

So many of us get to the *middle of the next step of our lives* and turn back. The tapes of other voices play in our ears—their opinions and judgments. They infect our spirits and we turn back. I can almost see God on the other side, urging us to take one more step. Instead, we turn around and do the same things we have always done, expecting failure and becoming morose about it.

God can do great things with us if we just come out of our boxes and walk across the bridge in front of us. God can't fit in the tiny spaces into which we have put ourselves. No, God is walking before us on rope bridge, showing us that the swaying, moving path on which we walk, though scary, will increase our faith and remind us that, *"with God all things are possible."*

We come to those rickety rope bridges over and over in our lives. Only if we risk stepping out and trusting God will we move from where we are to where God wants us to be.

Amen and amen.

DAY 33

WHEN YOUR HEART ACHES

Do not fret because of the wicked; do not be envious of wrongdoers,
for they will soon fade like the grass, and wither like the green herb.
—Psalm 37:1–2

There are words contained in the Bible that act as spiritual protein to strengthen our spiritual resolve and bolster our faith when life causes our hearts to ache.

I recently experienced such a day where I live, in Columbus, Ohio, when an arbitrator ruled to reinstate a white police officer into the Columbus Police Department who had been fired for kicking a young black man in the head as he lay on the ground in handcuffs. This same officer had been in the news before because of his involvement in the shooting death of another unarmed black man the year prior.

One more time, a black life was devalued and dishonored by law enforcement, carrying out a long-standing tradition. Throughout the history of this country, white law enforcement officers have metaphorically, and physically, stomped on the heads of black people, kicked us while we were down, and, at times, even executed us in cold blood, unconcerned about any legal consequences.

The pervasiveness of evil is not new; its stubborn persistence harkens to the words found in Psalm 37.

When will this evil of white supremacy finally fade and wither?

We do not have the answer to that question. All we know is that it has been going on forever.

Your heart can only ache for so long before the spirit urges you to take action, to step out of the fear and anger and risk *everything* in order to get *something*.

In her book, *At the Dark End of the Street*, Danielle L. McGuire highlights the black women who were behind the Montgomery bus boycott of 1955–1956. Black men certainly suffered under American apartheid, but so did black women. As they commuted to clean and cook for white families, these women suffered abuse from white bus drivers who had been deputized to "keep them in their place."

By the time Rosa Parks was arrested, black women had already organized enough to call for a boycott. Their aching hearts would not allow them to do anything less. They were tired of being humiliated. When Parks was arrested, they gathered at Alabama State University and, in one night, used a mimeograph machine to make fifty-two thousand fliers calling for a one-day boycott of all Montgomery buses. The next morning, they hit the streets, posting and passing out the fliers everywhere. They stood on street corners, put them in the windows of beauty parlors and barber shops, and nailed them to telephone poles.

Had it not been for the aching hearts of those black women, there would not have been a Montgomery bus boycott—certainly not one that lasted for 381 days!

Historical stories like these become both nurturing food and healing balm. But the beauty of their example, as well as other examples found in the Bible, is that they also strengthen the aching heart and cause us to hunger for action. Aching hearts become change agents in cutting down *"the green herb"* of injustice—be it in the form of racism, sexism, poverty, discrimination, or any other form of injustice. The aching heart cries from within and moves us to abandon our fetal position. We become human beings willing to do whatever it takes to be able to stand and walk with dignity.

When the report came that this Columbus police officer was reinstated into the police department, the universe must have gasped. The foot soldiers for justice drew in a long breath. The struggle continues—and it is exasperating. But if enough hearts are aching, even in this time when white supremacy is strutting amongst us with a renewed arrogance, many of us are being moved from complacency and fear toward courage and action.

Aching hearts will only take so much. They are a gift in the fight for justice. It is a weird thing to thank God for, but we can thank God anyhow because of the fact that aching hearts eventually cause us to stand up and risk everything when we can't take it anymore. Aching hearts compel us to release what we can no longer endure, and to work for what we thought we would never have.

Thank God, then, for aching hearts. They are a gift too precious for the work we have been called to do.

Amen and amen.

DAY 34
GOD IS OUR GUIDE

Listen, my elect ones, says the Lord; the days of tribulation are at hand, but I will deliver you from them. Do not fear or doubt, for God is your guide.
—2 Esdras 16:74–75

Y ou may have a hard time finding 2 Esdras in your Bible. It is a part of the Apocrypha, a group of books found in Christian Orthodox Bibles. It is not found in the Greek writings of the Bible but is included in the Appendix to the Latin Vulgate Bible, referred to as 4 Esdras. The fact that mainline Christians in this country do not often refer to the books of the Apocrypha does not take away the power of their words.

This message is comforting in a time when great comfort is needed. In spite of huge strides being made in the areas of racism and sexism, the actions of federal, state, and local governments often seem to be taking us back in history instead of progressing forward to a better future. A young man rapes a woman while she is unconscious and gets only six months jail time, with the possibility of parole in three months. The United States Supreme Court upholds extreme methods of search and seizure by law enforcement, further legitimizing racial profiling. The officer in Baltimore who faced the most serious charges in the death of Freddie Gray was acquitted by a judge. The water in Flint, Michigan, (and in other places) is still tainted with lead, and the federal government is in no hurry to provide the funds needed to provide clean water to the predominately African American community. The president issues racist remarks that act like a dog whistle for white supremacist factions of the American populace and for people with a deep-seeded appetite for hatred.

"The days of tribulation are at hand." Surely, that is so. Tribulation is very real for black and brown people, poor people, women, children of color, members of the LGBTQ community, and the loved ones of those struck down by gun violence. They know tribulation in the pits of their stomachs. American conservatives shout angrily about "radical Islamic terrorism," but ignore "radical Christian terrorism" that has been active from the formation of this nation.

"Do not fear or doubt, for God is your guide." Powerful words that sometimes fall hollow. It can often seem as though God is far away. Many, in the time of tribulation, scream for a clue that God is near, close by, involved in their pain, but often they cannot see, feel, or hear the "clue." God, our very present help in danger, seems to be distant and aloof.

In troubling times like these, when the hateful rhetoric seems to transcend all reason, faith, and belief, it is a challenge to not let fear or doubt get the upper hand. As we fight to maintain what is left of the Voting Rights Act, it will be hard to see our courts rule against the interests of black and brown citizens, while insisting that what they are doing is justice. As we watch our civic institutions sanction racism, xenophobia, corporate greed, abuse of women, and homegrown terrorism, it will be hard not to let fear, doubt, and bitterness take a front seat, and yet, we must do just that. We need to diligently push fear, doubt, and bitterness out of our spiritual spaces so the people who come to us wanting to know if God is real will be able to see a faith in our eyes and in our spirits. A faith that says, "Yes, God is real. God is our guide."

Of course, we can pray for the forces of evil to simply be crushed by a spiritual tsunami; we can pray for the forces of evil to be swept out to sea, never to return. But that will not happen. We know by now that sometimes God says "no" to the requests we make. God will not wash evil into the sea, but with our prayers, perhaps God will send more faith into our spirits and cause evil to lose some of its swag. God needs us to inhale God's Spirit and purpose, no matter how difficult things get. It's not a new exercise for oppressed people but it *is* an exercise guided, in the end, by God.

It is what keeps us sane in an insane world. And it is when we breathe deeply of the Spirit of God that we begin to feel God's deliverance.

In the end, and in the face of evil and oppression, God *is* our guide.

Amen and amen.

DAY 35
IN THE MIDST OF ENEMIES

For you have delivered my soul from death, and my feet from falling,
so that I may walk before God in the light of life.
—Psalm 56:13

On September 17–19, 2016, three bombs exploded and several unexploded devices were found in the New York/New Jersey metropolitan area. The bombings left thirty-one people wounded, but there were no fatalities or life-threatening injuries.

It was a difficult day to navigate.

The media went into 24/7 mode with information about the terrorist attacks. They lifted up the first responders as heroes, people who ran into danger to protect people. The man who made the bombs shot a police officer before he was himself shot by police. Both he and the officer survived. The narrative proclaimed the "bad" terrorists and the "good" police officers.

On September 16, 2016, just one day prior, a thirteen-year-old African American boy was fatally shot by police while playing with a BB gun. That same day, in Tulsa, Oklahoma, police shot an unarmed forty-year-old black man whose car had broken down while his hands were raised above his head.

For African Americans and other people of color, the pain is real. There is always a heaviness that sits on our chests like a sandbag, making it hard to breathe, whenever civil rights violations like this occur.

African Americans live behind enemy lines and in the midst of an enemy—white supremacy. Ever since we arrived in the New World, the stories of the atrocious treatment of black people are legion. For the longest time, black people have been internalizing the pain, the tears, the anger, and the frustration that have always been a part of living in America.

This enemy in our midst, white supremacy, is rearing its ugly head, bold and arrogant. Our people are still being lynched, no longer hung from trees but gunned down by police or languishing in a mass incarceration society. Even in the twenty-first century, the forces of evil that tormented our ancestors are still among us.

How do we manage our own tears and anger so that we can stand in the breach between honor and dishonor, righteousness and unrighteousness, mercy and injustice, love and hate?

The prophet Isaiah talks about a double portion of joy: *"Because their shame was double, and dishonor was proclaimed as their lot, therefore they shall possess a double portion; everlasting joy shall be theirs"* (Isaiah 61:7). We must ask that God inject us with a double portion of love, a double portion of divine attention and trust, enough to move the sandbag off our chests so we can breathe through the toxicity of hatred and bigotry. On this day, we ask that God "deliver our souls from death and our feet from falling." (See Psalm 56:13.)

Precious Lord, take our hands. We are tired, weak, and worn but we need You. On this day, we need You.

Amen and amen.

DAY 36
WILL GOD BRING JUSTICE?

When the poor and needy seek water, and there is none, and their tongue is parched with thirst, I the Lord will answer them, I the God of Israel will not forsake them. I will open rivers on the bare heights, and fountains in the midst of the valleys; I will make the wilderness a pool of water, and the dry land springs of water.
—Isaiah 41:17–18

On July 6, 2016, Alton Sterling and Philando Castile were executed by police officers in separate incidents. The next day, Dallas police officers were ambushed after a protest, killing five officers and injuring nine others. Soon afterward, a young woman came to me and asked, "Will God bring justice?" She was saddened, angered really, that someone had killed the police officers. "This is only going to make things worse for everyone but especially for us." Her question came only two weeks before three Baton Rouge police officers were also ambushed and killed.

This young woman was angry that the black men had been *executed* by police but that as soon as word of the deaths of the police officers hit the news, their deaths at the hands of the police slipped quietly into the background.

"It keeps happening and God isn't stopping it," she said. "Will God bring justice?"

In Isaiah 41, the prophet says, *"When the poor and needy seek water, and there is none, and their tongue is parched with thirst, I the LORD will answer them, I the God of Israel will not forsake them."*

The answer to the question has to revolve around what we think justice *looks like*, and what justice means to God. For African Americans, who have been plagued by racist hatred, policies, and practices from white Americans, justice has been elusive. God has not intervened to stop the arrogant willfulness of white supremacy. It seems that God has not stirred the souls and consciences of enough white people to motivate them to stand up and speak out against racism. God's *"still small voice"* (1 Kings 19:12 NKJV) has not compelled enough white people to enter the battlefield and fight for justice. God has allowed hatred to fester and grow.

On the other hand, God has given people of color a resolve and a strength that has been able to withstand *"the wiles of the devil"* (Ephesians 6:11). Though the emotional and spiritual wounds caused by the practice of white supremacy have been deep, and though the scars have been passed on from generation to generation, its evil existence has not vanquished black people.

Perhaps, to God, that is the beginning of justice. The hatred and bigotry, the out and out vitriol of white people, has, in effect, failed. Paul wrote, *"We are afflicted in every way, but not crushed; perplexed, but not driven to despair; persecuted, but not forsaken; struck down, but not destroyed; always carrying in the body the death of Jesus"* (2 Corinthians 4:8–10 ESV).

There are times when we feel like we are nearly crushed, close to giving into despair, forsaken and destroyed, but we are no different than our ancestors who felt the same way—and yet they kept on.

The evidence of God's justice might very well be that God has made us the "kept-on people," people who have "kept on" in spite of wanting to give up, in spite of not seeing even the hint of light amidst the darkness. We have "kept on," believing that *God is good*, and that belief has made us able to "hold on" and fight the Goliaths in our lives who laugh and mock us.

Like the shepherd boy David, we have five smooth stones called "keep on," "hold on," "press on," "lean on," and "depend on." If we gather those stones, keep them close, and use them as our weapons against the injustice that plagues us, perhaps we will see the kind of justice we yearn for. We can move on, picking up more stones whenever life demands it.

Amen and amen.

DAY 37
WALKING THE BRIDGE OF SIGHS

For in the day of trouble [God] will keep me safe in [God's] dwelling; [God] will hide me in the shelter of [God's] sacred tent.
—Psalm 27:5 NIV

In the book *Ambassadors of Reconciliation, Vol. II*, the authors tell the story of a man named Joe Avila, who recalls visiting Doge's Palace in Venice, Italy. Avila and his wife toured the prison dungeons of the medieval palace. Part of their tour included walking the Bridge of Sighs. This was the bridge every prisoner walked across after receiving his or her sentence for the crime they committed. The purpose of "the walk" was to allow the new prisoner to reflect on what he or she had done, to realize the consequences, and to "sigh." The book stated that, for the prisoner, "His sighs are his fears."

Years later, Avila himself was convicted of vehicular homicide in the death of a young woman after a drunken crash. The book details the remarkable story of how Avila learned about love and God's forgiveness through his ordeal. Avila recalled that after he was sentenced to twelve years in prison, he walked the quarter-mile-long underground tunnel at the Fresno County Jail. For convicted prisoners in that facility, said Avila, "that is where we reflect on what we have done and what is in store for us. I never want to walk down there again. That was my 'bridge of sighs.'"[12]

There are ways we can respond to our shortcomings that are helpful and ways that are counterproductive. To deny what we have done only keeps a wall between us and God, the God who can and will show us love and grace.

Our country lives in denial when it comes to racism and white supremacy. As a result, a wall stands between us and God, which keeps America from the healing and wholeness that comes from facing the truth, owning and embracing it, and thereby being released from its power over us. Denial of our shortcomings is counterproductive to our soul's health and, in the case of the United States, to the health of the nation.

The most effective way to deal with our shortcomings is to face them, to name them, and to place ourselves within the brokenness we have caused. Nobody likes to pay the price for what he or she has done, but we are all called to do so. When facing our shortcomings, we are forced to walk our "bridge of sighs." In that moment on the bridge, we are crestfallen, disappointed in ourselves, and above all,

---

12. Elaine Enns and Chad Myers, *Ambassadors of Reconciliation, volume II* (Maryknoll, NY: Orbis Books, 2009),

afraid of what lies ahead, how we will survive, and what or whom we will lose in the process. We fear facing the consequences of our actions. We walk and we sigh but when we walk with God, we do keep walking.

In facing our fears, we are liberated. Once we name them and take a deep breath, we begin to realize that while we must suffer now, that suffering is a part of our liberation, the road toward freedom. No person can put us down or shut us out because of what we have done. We gain the strength to tell our own story with remorse, conviction, and power. We are able to connect with others who have been afraid to approach the bridge. We no longer fear the consequences of what we have done because we are in the consequences and are still alive. We realize that some people will always hold what we have done against us, but we realize that there are many more who will not.

Joe Avila served his time. During his trial, he had an encounter with God and realized that instead of beating the system so that he could walk free, what he really desired was a redeemed life. He changed his plea from "not guilty" to "guilty," received a twelve-year sentence, endured the hatred and anger of his victims, walked through that long tunnel, served his time, and came out of prison seven years later a man made over by God.

Walking the Bridge of Sighs pushes our fears aside. Within us, fear will destroy us by stealing our capacity to trust God and understand how God works, especially in dark and tumultuous times. Walking that bridge of acceptance and accountability tells God that we truly believe that "*in the day of trouble, [God] will keep [us] safe in [God's] dwelling.*" In God's dwelling, there is pain as our weaknesses are exposed and excised but after some spiritual surgery, there is also healing, wholeness, and a joy that comes only when we realize how skillfully God excised our rotting parts and replaced them with new life, new possibilities, and new power and grace.

The Bridge of Sighs is a gift. For it, we are thankful.

Amen and Amen

DAY 38
A WALK ACROSS THE STREET

Come to me, all you that are weary and are carrying heavy burdens, and I will give you rest. Take my yoke upon you, and learn from me; for I am gentle and humble in heart, and you will find rest for your souls.
—Matthew 11:28–29

Despite the fact that mental illness is becoming a greater focus in public discourse, it is still a taboo subject in many Christian circles. It is seen as a challenge to the authority of God's healing powers and keeps many sufferers in the church from seeking help from mental health professionals.

I recently read a story about Linda Bishop, who had been diagnosed with bipolar disorder with psychosis as a young adult. Linda never accepted her diagnosis. She was prescribed medication for a while but abandoned taking it because it made her feel lethargic. Despite being institutionalized several times in her life, she resolutely refused to take her medication. She spiraled down into an abysmal darkness—experiencing homelessness and being arrested several times. She married, had a daughter, and was divorced. Linda abandoned her eleven-year-old daughter, saying she was going to look for the governor. Eventually, she was institutionalized again, this time for two years, still refusing to take any prescribed medication. She was finally released from the institution with nothing but the clothes on her back. Instead of calling her sister or her daughter, she wound up on a country road in New Hampshire, not far from where her family lived. She set up home in an abandoned house. She had nothing to eat, no heat, no electricity, and no water. She ate apples from trees in the yard until they were gone and it was too cold outside find any that she might have missed. During her four months in the house, she journaled about her feelings. Among her entries, she wrote, "God knows where I am."

Linda Bishop was fifty-one years old when she died in mid-winter but her badly decomposed body wasn't found until May.

Ironically, there had been help available nearby. Someone came to cut the lawn before winter. A family lived across the street. All she had to do was walk across the street. But that would have meant admitting why she was in that house, dirty, underweight, and showing signs of a serious mental disability. Unwilling to do that, she died alone.

Linda refused to walk across the street because she was a prisoner of demons within her own mind. I don't know if she prayed; the story didn't indicate, but she did refer to God in her writing. She acknowledged that if nobody else knew what she was going through, God did.

How many of us are prisoners of the demons in our own minds? We might not have a specific diagnosis of a mental illness but we recognize those demons within us who hold us captive. They prevent us from taking the necessary first steps toward the healing and restoration that God has in store for us. Help is frequently close by but because we don't want to admit we are hurting or struggling, we are unable to take that walk across the street, where help is willingly available.

Nobody escapes experiencing emotional turmoil; it is a part of life. Many of us have some degree of mental illness that we are not ready to accept, and others of us are on the brink. We pray, but if we cannot admit our true situation, even to God, we will be unable to find the help and strength we need.

How many of us put on masks, telling people we are perfectly fine when, in truth, we are very far from fine. Just as people who have heart problems or cancer or diabetes must seek medical help in order to find healing, we also need to seek help when the illness is in our spirits. In fact, we will never be as close to God as we need to be when we harbor our suffering in secret. Our pain will act as a barrier between us and God.

It is not God's will or desire that we suffer unduly—physically, emotionally, or spiritually. God is closer than across the street. God is with us and will not be angry if we seek help for our ailing spirits outside of the church. Prayer is always a viable tool but it works better when we use it in conjunction with the expertise and assistance of medical professionals. God does not want us to die of starvation in an abandoned house—literally or metaphorically. Rather, God says, *"Come to me, all you that are weary and are carrying heavy burdens, and I will give you rest."*

That rest is all the better when we take care of and tend to our afflicted spirits. Help is near; you need only to step out of your place of hiding and security, and, even while praying to God, let others know of your need for help. Healing and restoration are waiting, just across the street.

Amen and amen.

DAY 39

ON THE ELIMINATION OF ISOLATION

We, who are many, are one body in Christ, and individually we are members one of another.
—Romans 12:5

After creating the world, God said, *"It is not good that the man should be alone"* (Genesis 2:18). And so, God created woman.

In his book, *The Search for Common Ground*, Howard Thurman suggests that when an individual is cut off from the private and personal nourishment of other individuals, "the result is a wasting away, a starvation, a failure of his life to be sustained and nourished."[13] He later added, "The human spirit cannot abide the enforced loneliness of isolation. We literally feed on each other; where this nourishment is not available, the human spirit and the human body—both—sicken and die."[14]

Recently, there has been some discussion about the toxicity of loneliness. Health experts call it an epidemic as deadly as smoking fifteen cigarettes a day. It is more dangerous than obesity and a sedentary lifestyle. It is a major contributor to health problems such as hypertension and diabetes.

Our spirits cannot survive loneliness.

The reality of the prevalence of loneliness hit me when, some time ago, I talked with a woman whose daughter suffers from chronic depression. She is not treated for it and refuses to talk about it, but those of us who know her recognize that her spirit is

---

13. Howard Thurman, *The Search for Common Ground* (Hutchinson, IN: Friends United Press, 1986), 3.
14. Ibid.

lonely. "If she isn't here, visiting me, I know where she is," her mother said. "She runs home and goes to that little room."

In spite of the profundity of life, the beauty contained in it despite the difficulties, this young woman prefers four walls and a television to the outside world.

The question is, why do so many prefer lives of isolation instead of lives of community? Is it fear of rejection? Fear of failure or of being perceived as "less than?" Why is it that so many people prefer to retreat to their "little room" instead of going out into the world where they can commune with others?

God, in God's wisdom, knew the negative effect of loneliness. God knew that this entity called a "human being" must exist in community. God knew that human beings need love and acceptance, conversation and laughter, someone to talk to in bad times and someone to share in the good times. God knew.

The human race was created to make harmony in God's world—all voices, all ethnicities, all genders having a specific part in the symphony called life. God is the conductor, waving His spiritual baton to cue us when to crescendo and decrescendo. But whether we are increasing or decreasing, God expects us to remain a member of the orchestra. Our part is needed; no soloist is called for.

The poet John Donne wrote a poem about this. Forgive the exclusively male pronouns; it was written some four hundred years ago:

No Man Is an Island

No man is an island,
Entire of itself,
Every man is a piece of the continent,
A part of the main.

If a clod be washed away by the sea,
Europe is the less.
As well as if a promontory were:
As well as if a manor of thy friend's
Or of thine own were:
Any man's death diminishes me,
Because I am involved in mankind,
And therefore never send to know for whom the bell tolls;
It tolls for thee.

So many of us put ourselves in isolation for any number of reasons, in effect scraping minutes, days, hours, months, and even years off our lives. We choose to live in silence, but as the more contemporary poet Audre Lord says, "Your silence will not protect you."

Our silence and preference for isolation is a health risk and an affront to God, who created us so that we can participate in the orchestra of life. We ought to breathe in a cleansing breath of hope, which comes from God, and dare to leave the "little room." Life awaits us.

Amen and amen.

DAY 40

LEARNING TO THRIVE WHEN YOU HAVE BEEN MERELY SURVIVING

O taste and see that the LORD is good;
happy are those who take refuge in him.
—Psalm 34:8

Some people live full lives, but far too many others are merely surviving. They get up in the morning and slog through the same routine, returning home to prepare to do it all over again tomorrow. The "religion of creation," a phrase used by Wes Howard-Brook to describe the brand of faith God brought into this world, encourages us to lean on the arms and the teachings of Jesus, as opposed to the "religion of empire," which demands that we lean on the state. To lean upon the state is to merely survive, which is sometimes necessary, but too many of us have forgotten that God also wants us to push past the barriers of the state and to thrive. God wants us to *taste and see that the LORD is good.* God did not put us here merely to get by; God put us here to inhale the beauty of divine holiness and become inspired to be our best selves—warts, weaknesses, mistakes, and all.

It is risky to thrive. Thriving demands that we take chances. It demands that we learn to forgive ourselves and use our painful past as a roadmap to move forward. Thriving means we keep our ears and hearts inclined toward God, so we can know what and who we really are, thereby accepting and cherishing grace all the more.

The presence of Jesus is a lethal weapon against the propaganda the state wields—lies implying that those who are oppressed are somehow less than human, and thus, *deserving* of the second-class treatment they receive.

When we are in survival mode, we accept the state's propaganda, but something glorious happens when we look inside ourselves and, with the guidance of the Christ, we realize that despite our worst flaws, we are "*fearfully and wonderfully made*" (Psalm 139:14). At that precise moment, we hear the voice of God affirming us, regardless of what the world, our parents, or anyone else says about us. As we hear the divine affirmation of God, we understand that we can, and must, begin to use who and what we are to please God.

The late Rev. Dr. Katie Cannon wrote, "All interactions either encourage wholeness or brokenness. All experiences either nourish religious exposure to truth or snuff it out. Oneness with God progresses from outward life to the inward life, to outward life in community."[15] When we dare to look inward, risking being shocked by what we learn about ourselves, we put ourselves in position to be freed from the enslavement of self-hatred and self-doubt. We discover the wings that God gave us at the moment of our creation, and we decide that we are ready to fly.

I sometimes get the feeling that God is waiting—for me, surely, but also for all the other people—to get out of the safe places in which we have been surviving for so long. Nobody pleases God by surviving. Nobody experiences the joy of faith by deciding to stay safe. Nobody has enough strength to challenge injustice by deciding to stay safe. Deciding to remain safe can rightly be called *selfish* because we incubate our own insecurity rather than looking beyond ourselves and doing what God has gifted us to do to help "the least of these."

In this current political season, merely surviving is not enough. God needs us to thrive by trusting God in a way we never have before. Those who decide to survive will never move from the side of the pool but those who decide to thrive will high dive into the water of life, venturing so deep that they will have to lean on God in ways they never have before. In so doing, they will learn and rejoice that God's love for us and God's belief in us did not evaporate because of all the times we have fallen short.

---

15. Katie Cannon, *Black Womanist Ethics* (Eugene, OR: Wipf& Stock Publishers, 1988), 21.

God is waiting for more of us to jump into the water, daring to dive into places and spaces we have feared thus far. God will be there to help us breathe and survive in our new normal. But eventually, God will let us go and watch us as we surge forward on the currents, thriving as we never have before. And God will rejoice.

Amen and amen.

DAY 41
THE POWER AND PATHOS OF QUIET GRACE

Now may our Lord Jesus Christ himself and God our Father, who loved us and through grace gave us eternal comfort and good hope, comfort your hearts and strengthen them in every good work and word.
—2 Thessalonians 2:16–17

In the movie *12 Years a Slave*,[16] there is a scene where the child of a female slave, Eliza, is taken from her. The emotional distraught of this woman has never left my consciousness. In the book, Solomon Northrup, the free black man who was sold into slavery and remained a slave for twelve years, describes the day Eliza's child Emily was taken from her:

I have seen mothers kissing for the last time the faces of their dead offspring; I have seen them looking down into the grave, as the earth fell with a dull sound upon their coffins, hiding them from their eyes forever; but never have I seen such an exhibition of intense, unmeasured, and unbounded grief, as when Eliza was parted from

---

16. *12 Years a Slave*, directed by Steve McQueen (2013, Fox Searchlight Pictures).

her child. She broke from her place in the line of women, and rushing down where Emily was standing, caught her in her arms. The child, sensible of some impending danger, instinctively fastened her hands around her mother's neck, and nestled her little head upon her bosom. Freeman sternly ordered her to be quiet, but she did not heed him.[17]

Eliza's owner would not heed her plea to keep them together, and she cried out as her daughter was taken away, the two never to see each other again.

Eliza was never the same after that. She mourned with a heaviness that was palpable, a weight that was with her throughout the day, into the night, and then greeted her the next morning. She had no desire to live, but she lived on in spite of her pain. She carried on with what Katie Cannon described as "quiet grace." Cannon wrote, "'Quiet' is the qualifying word describing grace as a virtue in the moral agency of Black women. 'Quiet' acknowledges the invisibility of their moral character. Black women have never been granted the protective privileges that allow one to become immobilized by fear and rage."[18]

Quiet grace is a gift that cannot be overstated. Black women, and all women of color, have always had to draw from it in order to withstand the oppression that characterizes their lives. That said, we all have a need for it. Quiet grace is the antibiotic that fights the virulent, infected evil of oppression and gives us a strength we otherwise would not be able to utilize for our own benefit. It enables us to stand, "in spite of."

---

17. Solomon Northrup, *Twelve Years a Slave* (New York: Simon & Schuster, Inc.), 61.
18. *Black Womanist Ethics*, 125.

Years ago, I was under the dryer in a beauty shop when I saw, out of the corner of my eye, a man come barging in the front door. He walked straight to a woman who was sitting in the beautician's chair in front of me. Without a word, he took his fist and slammed it into the side of her face. As her head came back to its upright position, she slowly tilted her gaze up to look him in the eyes. She didn't spill a tear. She didn't say a word. He stood there with his fist balled to hit her again, but something about her gaze transformed that moment into something surreal. Her eyes never left his face; she was not at all threatened by his raised fist. She just looked at him, and moments later, he stormed out.

In retrospect, I believe that what we saw that day was quiet grace in action. To me, this woman was a warrior, a champion who had just staved off an enemy. On that day, I saw *quiet grace*, though I didn't know it at the time.

We all have things happen to us in this life that are wrong, unfair, and unjust. Who is it that makes it through such tough times? Who is it that can transform victimhood into victory? Quiet grace is a presence within us that lifts us when we need to be lifted, and it pushes us when we need to be pushed. It is a force that will not allow us to stay on the mat when we are down.

As black women have found the strength that comes from the gift of quiet grace, so might we all benefit by tapping into our own supply. We all have it. The purpose of quiet grace is to give us strength to carry on, strength to live and hope, and strength to believe that the evil around us is not the sum total of this human life.

Quiet grace is a most precious gift. It is something that has empowered oppressed people to withstand the slings and arrows of evil that have desired to wipe them out. As it has been an internal gift of power used in the past, so can it help all of us to get through the current struggles of our everyday lives.

Amen and amen.

DAY 42

EMBRACING THE THEOLOGY OF "SOMEBODINESS"

When you search for me, you will find me;
if you seek me with all your heart.
—Jeremiah 29:13

From the moment we are born, we become targets of an everpresent malevolent spirit that hovers over all of us. That spirit tells us that we are not worthy, not enough, not deserving of a good life. And that message is often delivered through the words and actions of those whom we love as well as those whom we do not even know.

Most of us have heard words like this: "You will never amount to anything!" Most often, they come from someone we know and love. They are deadly. Like a power drill, they bore a hole into our souls, providing a path for any other negative words or opinions to follow and infect our open wound of insecurity and self-loathing.

The feeling of being "nobody" or "not enough" follows us, sits with us, and reminds us of its presence. In the spiritual space of feeling like a "nobody," we minimize ourselves. How the world suffers because so many people are sitting in saucers of despair, unaware of their true worth!

Only as we deepen our relationship with God are we able to revive the antidote to the infectious disease called "insecurity." At first, most of us refuse to pray about it or ask God for help because we do not know how broken this wound has made us.

Slowly, we begin to perceive that something is wrong, off-balance. We admire people who have a sense of being "somebody," and we watch as they move and live in that knowledge. Eventually, we may tentatively seek God as never before. The words of the prophet Jeremiah give us God's promise: that we will find God when we search for God with all of our heart.

A judge once told me the story of when he asked a woman on trial for drug use to write an essay about her addiction. The woman began to read her essay aloud to the judge. "I am battling a terminal disease. Twenty-four years ago, I was told I had a terminal disease and had only months to live." The judge stopped her. "Can you read that last sentence again?" he asked. The woman repeated it and the judge asked, "Do you not hear what you said? Do you not see that you are so much more, and can do so much more, than you think you can? Do you realize that you have enormous strength? *Nobody* lives for 24 years with a diagnosis of a terminal disease." This woman was living in a place of fear, insecurity, self-pity, and "nobodiness," which provided the subliminal justification for her drug use.

The judge said that watching the woman's face was like watching a light come on. This poor soul had never considered her victories, her worth, or her strength, but had instead opted to live in a dungeon of despair for years. She believed she was nobody and so she had lived far below her spiritual and emotional capacity.

We are *somebody* because God made us so. It does not matter who has told us differently; their opinions do not trump God's genius in making us *somebody*. Our worth is not determined by our race, color, gender, sexuality, emotional health, or physical illness; it is not determined by the thickness of our lips or the width of our hips; it is not determined by our level of education or the jobs we do. Our worth was created and built into us at the moment of our conception.

We recognize moments when we wrestle away from feeling like nobody and begin to understand that we are somebody. We can feel it. We know when some stubborn part of us has been released and we begin to embrace the theology of "somebodiness." We live the words of the cherished hymn: "I once was lost, but now am found. T'was blind but now I see"!

We are somebody, no matter what.

Amen and amen.

DAY 43
WE CAN DO ALL THINGS

When [Jesus] saw that they were straining at the oars against an adverse wind, he came towards them early in the morning, walking on the sea. He intended to pass them by. But when they saw him walking on the sea, they thought it was a ghost and cried out; for they all saw him and were terrified. But immediately he spoke to them and said, "Take heart, it is I; do not be afraid."
—Mark 6:48–50

Whenever the summer temperatures soar, both my daughter and my dogs turn to me with miserable looks on their faces. That's when I remind them, "It will be okay. I grew up without air conditioning and I made it. We'll be all right."

Growing up, the summers in Detroit were ferocious. We had one fan that was placed facing out in an upstairs window of what we called "the middle room." Daddy swore it was blowing the hot air out of the house, but I, for one, could not tell if the fan was doing any good at all. At night, we slept in our underwear on sticky sheets, finding the dry spot in the bed and staying there, and rotating the pillow over and over again to find the "cool spot." Eventually, we drifted off to sleep and, lo and behold, we awakened the next morning to find that we had made it through the night.

"Making it through" is what we do in difficult times. Our lives are unstable. The circumstances of our lives ebb and flow like restless seas; there are low tides when things are calm and bearable, but then there are the high tides, when we struggle to keep our heads above water to survive. The cycles of instability in life never go away, but we make it through.

Knowing and hearing that things will be all right—that we will make it through—has been a source of power for marginalized people. In a sense, being marginalized and oppressed carries its own gifts. The marginalization teaches that trouble will not last. Trouble is a high tide, a hot and sticky summer day with no air conditioning. We may be miserable but trouble is not terminal, not in and of itself.

If only God would make life easier. If only there were no such things as injustice or cruelty or hatred. But God doesn't work that way. Of course, our misery does not amount to much when you consider what our forebears endured. Can you imagine dealing with the hot extended summers of the Deep South when you are a slave picking cotton?

At least summer is only few months long. Our current political season is just as hot, only it never seems to end. The atmosphere is forever thick with the humidity of bigotry, hatred, misogyny, and economic distress—but we have endured hard political times before. In the midst of the heat, there is God. Always, there is God. If we look for God, if we are *"straining at the oars against an adverse wind"* as Jesus's disciples were, we will make it through, once again. The only relief from the oppression we struggle against is the promise that God is truly good—all the time.

If we remember that, practice that, and teach that, we will all make it through. We all will be all right.

Amen and amen.

DAY 44
ESCAPING DECEPTION

"The time has come," [Jesus] *said. "The kingdom of God has come near. Repent and believe the good news!"*
—Mark 1:15 NIV

I often quote Howard Thurman because he is a hero to me. This morning, I was struck by some words he wrote: "The penalty of deception is to *become* a deception, with all sense of moral discrimination vitiated. A man who lies habitually becomes a lie, and it is increasingly impossible for him to know when he is lying and when he is not."[19]

We all prefer deception at some time in our lives. The truth is too difficult to face and accept. We find the truth distasteful and it does nothing to bolster our spirits. So we deceive ourselves. We believe that what we want to be is what is. We think more highly of ourselves than we ought. We believe that what we want to look like is how we actually look.

---

19. Howard Thurman, *Jesus and the Disinherited* (Boston, MA: Beacon Press, 1976), 65.

We do not want to believe that our son or daughter may be on drugs, and so we deceive ourselves into thinking that what we are seeing is not the truth. We do not want to believe that a spouse is cheating or that we are not important in the eyes of someone close to us, and so we deny it.

Denial is one of the principal components of deception. If we deny the truth, then for us, the truth does not exist.

We see denial and deception in the halls of government as key figures refuse to acknowledge the corruption, the hatred, and the oppression, which only leads to more and more deception. Many American citizens are party to both the deception and the denial, refusing to see that what is going on is damaging America in a way that will last for generations. Those in Congress, for whatever reason, deny that our Constitution is being chipped away, piece by piece. They are complicit in the blatant abuse of power that is being exhibited by their acquiescence of it.

The penalty of deception is to become a deception. So many Christians, for political gain, are denying the core tenets of Christianity, convincing themselves that they are walking in alignment with the Christ. In so doing, they have become a deception. Christians have become silent in the face of injustice. They have refused to hear the cries of the suffering, and refused to see their pain or address their needs. It is this rampant deception that has pushed so many people away from the church and away from God.

How do we stop deceiving ourselves? How do we gain the courage to look at ourselves and see who we really are and accept what we really believe? How do we escape "being" deceivers and begin to walk in the truth that will set us and others free?

Perhaps our work begins with an understanding of the "good news." In the first chapter of the gospel of Mark, "good news" is phrase found in both verse 1 and verse 15. Mark begins his gospel by stating: *"The beginning of the good news about Jesus the Messiah, the Son of God...."* Then, in verse 15, Jesus responds to the arrest of John the Baptist by going to Galilee: *"The time has come,"* he said. *"The kingdom of God has come near. Repent and believe the good news!"*

What, in light of a consideration of deception, is the *"good news"*? Perhaps we have truncated the meaning of *good news* and made it a self-serving principle that merely provides us with assurance that we are safe from eternal damnation. The words of Scripture do not seem to support that belief, as Jesus Himself says, *"Not everyone who says to me, 'Lord, Lord,' will enter the kingdom of heaven"* (Matthew 7:21 NIV). It seems that Jesus understood that human beings have a great capacity to manipulate the truth of God's words to favor their own situations.

But what if the "good news" is that, no matter what, God is with us? What if it means that we no longer have to pretend that everything is okay? What if the "good news" is the counter-message to the message the world tells us? What if it means that *who we are* and *what we have done* does not keep God from loving us? What if it requires that we are engaged in the action of repenting, literally, "turning toward God," on a continual basis? What if the only way to escape being a deception is to kill off those lying parts of ourselves, like weeds that keep springing up in the garden and must continuously be pulled on an ongoing basis?

Nobody wants to be a deception. But once we recognize and face our own deceptions, we can make changes. Until we do that, deception cripples us, keeping us from joy, peace, and fulfillment.

Letting go of the *need* to live in deception frees us up, and thus, makes us true workers in and for the kingdom.

Let us stop being content with being deceptions and begin to hold on to the "good news"—that whatever the truth is about us, God is always there.

Amen and amen.

DAY 45
OUT OF BABYLON

By the rivers of Babylon—there we sat down and there we wept when we remembered Zion.
—Psalm 137:1

Sometimes, we find ourselves in a place that violates everything in which we have always believed. That place feels cold and odd and uncomfortable; we writhe in discomfort and yearn for what we used to know. Nothing feels right. Though we try to go through the motions of the life we have known, we feel an isolation and distance, sometimes even from God.

The ancient Jews knew this feeling in their exile to Babylon. First, the Babylonians set siege to Jerusalem, burning, destroying, and killing most of what the Jews loved. The survivors were taken captive and carried off to Babylon. There they sat, forlorn and distressed, missing their beloved Jerusalem. The prophet Ezekiel was among the exiles, mourning with his people along the banks of the Chebar River.

But there is something striking about the Babylonian exile that perhaps we don't think about often. Yes, the Jews mourned, *"By the*

rivers of Babylon—there we sat down and there we wept when we re-
membered Zion. On the willows there we hung up our harps. For there
our captors asked us for songs, and our tormentors asked for mirth, say-
ing, 'Sing us one of the songs of Zion!'" (Psalm 137:1–3).

How absolutely insensitive, we might say, for those who cap-
ture us and steal our joy to dare us to call on our God! And yet,
the history of the Babylonian captivity shows that the Jews never
let go of their God. They never stopped believing, never stopped
worshiping, and never stopped acknowledging that God is God, no
matter what.

They sang the Lord's song in a strange land.

Being in Babylon is not comfortable or fun, whether it is because
of our own doing, the oppression of others, or a combination of both.
Under the pressure of evil, with individuals or government threatening our ability to thrive, there is a tendency to give up. It seems easier
for some; we give in to powers that seem greater than God.

But there is no power greater than God. Even amidst horrific
pain and suffering, God is sovereign. Yes, we have questions about
how a good God, a sovereign God, a God who loves us all, could
allow such suffering—and no, we will never have answers to those
questions—but history tells us that those who *sing the Lord's song in
a strange land* will increase their strength and their capacity to bear
the burden of suffering. Those who refuse to curse God and die, as
Job's wife advised him to do, ultimately get through the horrific pain
that injustice and evil cause, even though, at the end of that journey,
they are not the same.

We are not supposed to be the same. Babylon changes us.

I can remember my own mother singing at the kitchen sink,
looking out the window as she worked, singing, "Jesus, keep me

near the cross." She sang it with such passion that I would start singing it, too. We were an African American family with five kids and two parents struggling to make ends meet. I imagine there were times when she and my father did not know how they were going to make it.

Babylon.

But my mother would sing, that song and others, and we often joined her. In America, we were in exile. In America, we had to remember that white supremacy was not the boss of us, and that, always, God was there.

Babylon.

The Jews in exile never stopped worshiping God. They never let Babylon become sovereign over them. They survived and eventually thrived. They did so well that when deliverance came, some did not want to go back to Jerusalem. God had turned their mourning into dancing. God did it then; God can do it now.

Getting out of Babylon means turning to God like we never have before. Getting out of Babylon means singing a new song to the Lord every day, in such a way that others will want to join us.

Babylon is not forever. God is.

Amen and amen.

DAY 46
WHEN GOD CLOSES A DOOR

O sing to the Lord a new song; sing to the Lord, all the earth. Sing to the Lord, bless his name; tell of his salvation from day to day. Declare his glory among the nations, his marvelous works among all the peoples.

For great is the Lord, and greatly to be praised; he is to be revered above all gods.
—Psalm 96:1–4

Sometimes, God closes doors.

God gives you a hint. You can feel the spiritual nudging within you, telling you that something is up. You try to ignore it, but you cannot. A "God-nudge" is persistent and can become annoying. When God is trying to tell us something, or when God is getting ready to change something in our lives, God needs us to know that it is no accident.

Sometimes we like what God does, but at other times, we do not. We rejoice when God opens doors to give us fresh, new blessings! God opening doors is one of the best things that can happen to anyone.

But just as God opens doors, God also closes them. We don't like that much. Why did God just close that door? It is at these times that we have to retreat into our spirits to find peace in spite of our angst over what God has done.

When God closes a door, there is always a reason.

Sometimes, God has to break your heart in order to strengthen your spirit, and thus, your faith. Yes, *God does break our hearts sometimes*. It's not always the devil. God is in control, ultimately, and for every broken heart God causes, there is something that God is trying to strengthen. When God closes doors, it breaks our hearts, but when it happens, we can trust and believe that God did not want us to go through that door—not one more time. Sometimes, the doors we go through make our spirits and our faith weaker. Sometimes, we try to make do with a situation that is not meant to be.

In love, then, God closes the door. God loves us too much to keep letting us go to a place that is not good for us. God knows that if the wrong door is not closed, we might never be inclined to search for the right door.

God does this because there is always a "right" door.

British Baptist preacher Charles Spurgeon wrote a sermon entitled, "David's Prayer in the Cave." He wrote, "Is it not a curious thing that whenever God means to make a man great, He always first breaks him into pieces?" He continues, "Have none of you ever noticed, in your own lives, that whenever God is going to give you an enlargement and bring you out to a larger sphere of service, or to a higher platform of spiritual life, you always get thrown down?"

Spurgeon said, "Do not wonder if you go by the way of the cave." Why? Because, "if God would make you greatly useful, He must teach you how to pray. And," he writes, "the man whom God would greatly honor must always believe in God when he [she] is at his [her] wits' end." And finally, "in order to greater usefulness, many a man [woman] of God must be taught to stand alone."

Spurgeon said a lot more in that sermon, but those three points are good places to start when trying to understand why God has shut a door in your life. It is not a bad thing, though it is painful. And it may be that some evil has caused it to close but, more often than not, it is God breaking our hearts in order to strengthen our spirits, our faith, and our capacity for the work still before us.

There is grace waiting on the other side of the closed door. There is grace and love and a new strength that will inspire us to sing new songs, which God requires. "Sing unto the Lord a new song" even as you stand looking at that impenetrable and immovable door. God might have closed it recently, even as you were preparing to enter it one more time, but believe and know that it is not a bad thing, but, rather, an act of love that will help you do and be what God has called you to do and be.

Amen and amen.

DAY 47
THE POWER OF EMBARRASSMENT

And after you have suffered for a little while, the God of all grace, who has called you to his eternal glory in Christ, will himself restore, support, strengthen, and establish you.
—1 Peter 5:10

When I was a child, I went overboard in trying to be "good."

For most of my childhood, I never felt "good enough." The man my mother married adopted me so that I would share the same last name as my other siblings, but his family never accepted me. Kids being kids, my new siblings would remind me that I didn't belong. I was an outsider and they let me know it.

I compensated for this by trying to be a "good girl," what we would today call a "goody-two-shoes." The problem was, nobody is that good and trying to be that good only breeds resentment among your peers. I didn't know all that, so I redoubled my effort to become "the best kid ever."

I was chosen to be a part of an elite group called "the grass patrol." We, the chosen ones, were singled out for our good behavior. We were let out of class early, given lime green safety patrol belts, and stood at our posts in front of an area that had been freshly seeded, holding our arms out to keep kids on the sidewalks and off the turf.

All was well until one day, a boy named Dana Henderson (yes, I still remember his name) approached me and stood defiantly inches in front of me. Dana was skinny, talked funny, and was not popular. But on this day, he was going to prove himself at my expense. He accused me of thinking I was better than everyone else and he pushed me.

I stood my ground, arms held out, guarding the grass seed.

When he saw I wasn't afraid of him, he pushed me several more times and then spit in my face.

It was over. Before I knew what I was doing, I jumped him, green patrol belt and all, and knocked him to the ground. I was lost in a rage of fury, pummeling his body, when all of a sudden, I felt myself being lifted off the ground. It was the principal. Mr. Corgiat looked at me with utter disgust. As if that wasn't bad enough, my embarrassment was made complete when the crowd of kids who had gathered to watch the fight began to laugh and point at me. Someone said, "Look at Goody-Two-Shoes!"

I was "written up" and joined the ranks of the ne'er-do-wells. I carried that embarrassment for years.

I was thus stunned when I read words of Abraham Heschel, who wrote, "Embarrassment, loss of face, is the beginning of faith; it will make room within us." What a profound thought! Make room for what? Make room for God, for God's voice, for God's direction. Heschel said, "Embarrassment is meant to be productive; the end of embarrassment would be a callousness that would mark the end of humanity."

Heschel claimed that religion begins with embarrassment. Religion means challenge, not complacency. Challenge means overcoming our adjustment to conventional notions, to mental clichés.

In life, we are embarrassed more often than we like to admit. It is not a pleasant experience, but its spiritual and educational value is something we should not take for granted. If, in our embarrassment, we can reach out to God, God will fill us with the spiritual strength which we earn by attrition and that is often the result of having done something of which we are not proud.

I never fought on the school grounds again. When I would see Dana Henderson, I would just lower my head and keep going because—truth be told—I was *still* furious with him. I endured the cackling of my classmates who were glad that "goody-two-shoes" had fallen, and I withstood the punishment meted out by both the school and my mother, who was totally unimpressed by my behavior.

In our walk with God, we will fall; we will be embarrassed. But if, as Heschel said, "embarrassment is the beginning of faith," then perhaps we should handle our embarrassments with a feeling of hope and purpose.

In the moment of our embarrassment, our dry spirits can reach for God, who will hydrate us and provide the encouragement we need to learn from it instead of fretting and regretting a moment in our life that is long gone. In the end, our embarrassing moments are gifts that provide us with more strength and wisdom.

Amen and amen.

DAY 48
THE POWER OF RELEASING GRIEF

The light shines in the darkness, and the darkness did not overcome it.
—John 1:5

There is nothing quite so life-giving as a Black church service in which we celebrate "in spite of." Years ago, I interviewed one of the sisters of Bishop John Richard Bryant who said and explained to me that "Sunday morning is about grief-release." The statement struck me and has stayed with me.

In church, we sing, we shout, and we stomp, as if to stomp out all the craziness, evil, and injustice around us. Sunday morning is about opening our hearts and spirits to the One who is greater than all that is in the world.

Throughout history, oppressed people have survived because of knowing how to release the grief that comes from fighting the never-ending battle for justice, the grief that comes from being denied justice from the judicial system, and the grief that comes from being subjugated by people—in our case, primarily by white men—who do not believe we are equals on this earth. Mothers of young black men gunned down by people—either by police or by a criminal on the street—have perfected the art of grief release. The tears they shed during worship are often dually aligned with our grief and with a hope and a joy that we know we cannot ever lose.

In spite of great efforts to extinguish our hope, our faith, and our existence, there has always been God, the God of the light that *"shines in the darkness"* and cannot be put out. Our God shines light into our darkness and breathes the Holy Spirit into our spirits, giving us the strength to press on.

God has put within us an amazing spirit that equips us to move through our grief; we do not lose our grief but we learn to use it in a life-giving way. It is part of the wonder of how God takes care of us.

Astrophysicist Neil deGrasse Tyson shared a fascinating physical reality that illustrates the untouchable power of God. On an Internet chat, he claimed, "Within one linear centimeter of your lower colon there lives and works more bacteria (about 100 billion) than all humans who have ever been born."[20] He said, "The atoms that make up the human body are traceable to…stars when, unstable in their later years, collapsed and exploded, scattering their enriched guts across the galaxy. Guts made of carbon, nitrogen, oxygen, and all the fundamental ingredients of life itself."[21]

The wonder and power of God is beyond our comprehension. Our grief is large, but not larger than God. Our grief responds to the prodding of God, who knows our grief but also knows the power that has been planted with us to help us overcome that grief.

The psalmist says, *"O Lord, you have searched me and known me…. Even before a word is on my tongue, O Lord, you know it completely…. Where can I go from your spirit? Or where can I flee from Your presence?"* (Psalm 139:1, 4, 7). This God knows our grief and this God determined a long time ago that our grief would not minimize us but would instead strengthen us to stand up and to stay up.

The words and actions of oppressive powers cause our people much pain, fear, and angst. We are not sure what tomorrow will

---

20. https://www.reddit.com/r/IAmA/comments/qccer/i_am_neil_degrasse_tyson_ask_me_anything/c3wguoh/ (accessed July 7, 2019).
21. https://www.youtube.com/watch?v=9D05ej8u-gU#action=share (accessed July 7, 2019).

bring. We are grieving as we listen to what our nation's leaders say about us, grieving as we stand witness to the silence of people who say they know God but who allow evil to reign, and grieving as we realize that much of the work we have done over the past fifty or more years is assaulted and undone. We feel a deep sense of fatigue from having grieved for so long.

But, as we have done in the past, we will work in that grief and release it so that we can continue to fight against the forces that threaten us. In our spiritual colons are billions of life-giving cells that have kept us thus far and that will keep us going forward. We have a power that that has been hardened by the grief within our souls. It has always kept us alive and it always will.

Amen and amen.

DAY 49
THE POWER OF MOVING

Jesus said to [the paralyzed man], "Stand up, take your mat and walk."
—John 5:8

What do you do when you are in a bad space? How do you survive?

One of the best things you can do is keep moving.

Movement says that you have hope in your spirit, and hope is the driver that helps us out of the dark spaces in our lives and into the light. Sitting still is not an option. Movement is a lifesaver; it allows our spiritual selves to receive the nutrients that keep us alive. Movement increases our spiritual circulation, which is necessary for life. The moment we stop moving, stop looking for light, stop looking for answers, we put ourselves in a cast that weakens our bodies because of non-use.

It is not difficult to understand this concept when you consider what happens if you do not use your muscles. They atrophy. They get weaker and weaker until they are of no use. Muscles need to expand and contract in order to remain viable and to keep the strength needed to support us. After knee or hip replacement, even after open-heart surgery, patients are made to get up and move. When athletes suffer horrific injuries, they are made to get up and begin moving as soon as possible.

Sometimes, the tendency not to move—or the inability to move—is caused by disease. One such disease is polio. An uninvited and unwelcomed virus enters the body via the mucous membranes, caused by oral contact or fecal matter. Once it reaches the nervous system, it destroys nerve cells that activate skeletal muscles. Nerve cells do not regenerate, and the result is permanent muscle weakness or paralysis. Most often, the legs are compromised but severe infections can occur throughout the body, causing quadriplegia and hampering the ability to breathe. I will never forget seeing pictures of polio victims in "iron lungs" in order to breathe.

In our own lives, there have been times when we have been injured or invaded by uninvited and unwelcome spiritual, social, or cultural viruses. Just because you believe in God doesn't mean you are immune to the threats around you. The winds of treachery are everywhere; they long to cut you off and cut you down. They would like to see you stop moving and give in to their power.

Our goal must always be to keep our eyes on the prize, be that personal growth, spiritual maturity, or cultural and societal justice.

In the movie, *The Revenant*,[22] Leonardo DiCaprio's character never stopped moving, in spite of being attacked and mauled by a bear, in spite of freezing temperatures, and in spite of being alone. He just kept on moving. It was hard; he was so injured and broken that he wanted to lie down and die. But he had a mission, a purpose, and he was bound and determined to honor his goal. His determination to do that allowed him to survive and, ultimately, to thrive. He was not the same at the end of his perilous journey; he was better. He was stronger. He had faced situations that tried hard to paralyze his soul and spirit, yet he was victorious.

My prayer is that you will keep moving, that you will not allow the viruses in your personal, social, religious, and political life make your spiritual muscles atrophy and take away your ability to breathe. I pray you will be able to exhale the toxicity of evil and oppression and inhale the Spirit of God, your Source of power.

Standing still is not an option.

Amen and amen.

DAY 50
THE POWER OF DOING LITTLE THINGS

> [Jesus] *put before them another parable: "The kingdom of heaven is like a mustard seed that someone took and sowed in his field; it is the smallest of all the seeds, but when it has grown it is the greatest of shrubs and becomes a tree, so that the birds of the air come and make nests in its branches."*
> —Matthew 13:31–32

---

22. *The Revenant*, directed by Alejandro G. Iñárritu (2015, 20th Century Fox).

We often do not understand how it is the "little things" that make the biggest impact on the lives of people around us. Those little things can be positive or negative—words, gestures, attitudes, body language, all of them count. It is unfortunate that, often, we do not appreciate or recognize their power.

I heard a story on NPR about Sylvia Bullock, who was a minister, raising a son on her own. He was a kid, doing what kids do, and when he was fifteen, he stole a car. Though it was his first offense, he was tried as an adult and was sentenced to eight years in prison.

He was afraid, of course, and so was his mother. He had heard horror stories of what prison was like, so he concentrated on survival. His mother wanted him to survive as well but she also wanted him to know that, no matter what, she still loved him. So, while he concentrated on surviving, she concentrated on staying connected.

The loss of her son to the criminal justice system ate at her and she grew depressed. Nothing seemed to matter anymore except staying connecting with her son and making the connection stronger than it had ever been before.

She wrote her son letters, consistently, for the entire time he was in prison. The letters meant everything to her son and gave him something to look forward to. In her letters, she bared her soul. For her, writing was the only way to honor her intention to stay connected.

When her son was released from prison, Sylvia Bullock—*Rev. Sylvia Bullock*—was there. She had been a minister in the way that counts most, by doing the "little things" for her biggest blessing, her son. Her embarrassment at having a son incarcerated was sent to the back of the bus. If anyone was going to save her child, it would be her, with the help of God. She wrote letters. She called the wardens. And she never lost hope or confidence in her son.

After her son's release, he started a business that makes it easier for families and inmates to communicate. His mother is the chief operating officer. He is being the man that she knew he was, and more. She was not about to let a system dictate who her son was. It was through doing the little things that she communicated love, compassion, and the reality of God.

The story made me think about what little things I could be doing for others, and it also made me do inventory of the little things I do that affect others in a negative way. God has made no mistakes, and even if nobody ever tells us that, it is something we should know.

Sylvia Bullock knew it. She knew she was not a mistake and she sure knew her son was not a mistake. She knew that the crime he had committed was not the definition of who he was. She knew that the love she communicated by doing little things like writing letters and calling the warden would let her son know that, in this world, he mattered and had worth. She refused to let the "big thing"—the prison system—take her son and shred his spirit.

It is the little things that change our environment and our world. It is the little things that can make crooked places straight and the rough places smooth. It is the little things that will make this world what God wants it to be.

Amen and amen.

DAY 51

THE POWER OF VISION

Write the vision; make it plain on tablets, so that a runner may read it. For there is still a vision for the appointed time; it speaks of the end, and does not lie. If it seems to tarry, wait for it; it will surely come, it will not delay.
—Habakkuk 2:2–3

When I was a church pastor, I directed the choir for years. I used to frequently remind them, "One day, we're going to Carnegie Hall!" I was joking, of course, but the truth I was conveying was that we were not "just" a church choir. We were a body of musicians, determined to sing a joyful song that would bring God's healing, empowerment, and inspiration to anyone who listened.

I could envision us in Carnegie Hall. I could envision us giving a concert in our church accompanied by a full orchestra. I could envision the women in long black dresses and the men in tuxedos. I envisioned those things every day.

And then it happened. Not Carnegie Hall, but the concert. It was out of the blue, only it wasn't. I stood in my church, some members of the Columbus Symphony Orchestra sitting in chairs with their instruments and music stands, and the choir standing on risers in front of me. I looked down at a full orchestral score and it hit me. *The vision had come to fruition.* I remembered the words of Habakkuk: *"Write the vision; make it plain on tablets, so that a runner may read it. For there is still a vision for the appointed time; it speaks of the end, and does not lie. If it seems to tarry, wait for it; it will surely come, it will not delay"* (Habakkuk 2:2–3).

I had forgotten the power of vision. I had forgotten that, within all of us, there is the power of vision. What we see, our spirits see as well, and our spirits take over and begin to carry us toward the vision we have seen. We are working, yes, but our spirits are working with us, concurrently. We may find ourselves straining to climb steep mountains, wandering in dark spaces, or struggling in waters too deep for our feet to touch bottom, but the vision within us keeps us moving. Once that vision takes hold of our spirits, our path has been navigated and our spirits keep us moving toward the goal.

Visions are not realistic; they are almost always grander than anything that makes sense to us or anyone around us. They tell us that "the impossible" may be possible after all, but subject to interruption by the human spirit that has been watered and nurtured by God. Visions are sometimes so big that we dare not say a word to anyone about what we have seen for fear of being ridiculed, yet they are simultaneously so exciting that we frequently cannot keep them to ourselves.

When trouble comes, we sometimes shut down and cannot see anything other than our own distress. When that happens, we have compromised one of the functions of God. God celebrates our willingness to risk believing in all the things God can make happen.

When we see mountains that are too high to climb alone but we begin the journey anyway, God grins because it allows us to enter into a deeper relationship with God, one that will increase our faith *and* allow God to insert glory and strength into everything we do.

I had forgotten the power of vision, and many of us do the same at certain periods of our lives. I had forgotten that having a vision is, for God, an exciting thing; the vision coming to life within us must be like a birth experience for God. God sees the vision grow and then burst out of us because it can no longer be contained. Vision is so powerful that we often do not consider its power; such extreme magnificence is too great for us.

On this day, I thank God for reminding me of when I stood and looked down at that orchestral score. I thank God for reminding me of the violins and violas and cellos, the harp and percussion and bells, the trumpets, trombones, cornets, and flutes. There was an *orchestra* in my little church! I thank God for reminding me of the expectant eyes of that choir as I raised the baton for the first downbeat.

I thank God for vision.

And I pray that our eyes will *see* what we dare not even share with anyone—not yet. The struggles we have been through will make the vision greater, and though it tarries, it will surely come.

Amen and amen.

DAY 52
MOURNING INTO DANCING

You have turned my mourning into dancing; you have taken off my sackcloth and clothed me with joy, so that my soul may praise you and not be silent. O LORD my God, I will give thanks to you forever.
—Psalm 30:11–12

There are particular realities the shepherd must know, however unpleasant they may be. The shepherd is required to guide the sheep past dark and dangerous places because, if the sheep stumble into them, they will lose sight of the shepherd and die. When we human "sheep" are swallowed up by the darkness, we begin to doubt the power of God and, ultimately, lose hope.

One of those dark places is found at the intersection of race and religion, which, as James Baldwin said, "are fearfully entangled in the guts of this nation."[23] Baldwin said, "Both the white fundamentalist minister and the deputy are Christians—*hard-core* Christians…. Both believe they are responsible, the one for divine law and the other for natural order. Both believe that they are able to define and privileged to impose law and order; and both, historically and actually, know that law and order are meant to keep me in my place."[24]

It is an amazing and tenuous job placed on the shoulders of the shepherd. In the midst of the darkest hours, the shepherd has to determine the direction of the light, primarily for his or her own personal survival, and then the shepherd must guide others away from the trap and toward the glow of wholeness that is Christ Jesus.

As we deal with the phenomenon of law enforcement officers, mostly white but not all, indiscriminately gunning down and killing black and brown people, we are charged with the responsibility of finding the Light.

We are all mourning. The prophet Jeremiah says that God will turn our mourning into dancing, but we are not dancing yet. To dance is to move toward the Light; to dance is to move toward God. The dancing is not something that indicates we are minimizing our pain or the pain of our sheep; the dancing that comes from mourning enables us to cross over the hot coals of racism, sexism,

---

23. James Baldwin, *The Cross of Redemption: Uncollected Writings* (New York: Pantheon, 2010), 200.
24. Ibid., 161–162.

homophobia, and crony capitalism toward the cooling Light that is the Spirit of Christ Jesus.

We know the coded language. We know what it means when one political candidate calls him or herself the "law and order" candidate." I think of what that phrase has meant historically in this nation, and what "law and order" actually means, according to Baldwin's observations.

But I also enter into the dance—over the very hot coals—and declare that we will not stop dancing until all that is wrong has been made right. No politician, no government, no evil and immoral policy can keep us "in our place" if we continue moving toward God. It may not happen in my lifetime or in yours, but if we continue to dance toward God, over those coals, we will teach our sheep to do the same, and we will experience how God has the ability to turn our mourning into dancing, evil notwithstanding. We will dance.

Amen and amen.

DAY 53
WHY WE WRESTLE

Jacob was left alone; and a man wrestled with him until daybreak. When the man saw that he did not prevail against Jacob, he struck him on the hip socket; and Jacob's hip was put out of joint as he wrestled with him. Then he said, "Let me go, for the day is breaking." But Jacob said, "I will not let you go, unless you bless me." So he said to him, "What is your name?" And he said, "Jacob." Then the man said, "You shall no longer be called Jacob, but Israel, for you have striven with God and with humans, and have prevailed."
—Genesis 32:24–28

In order to move to a different place, a better place, a safer space, we must wrestle.

It does not seem right or fair. If God is with us, you'd think that wrestling should not be necessary, at least not ongoing wrestling. In Genesis 32:22–32, Jacob wrestles with God and we get the impression from this passage that his life was smooth sailing afterward.

The story belies the fact that wrestling with God, and with God's divine will, is a constant in life. There are no easy answers to the questions we struggle with. There is no easy roadmap to avoiding conflicts with injustice. As we seek God, we often find that the demonic angels (a description used by the late Vincent Harding) are always around us, taunting, tempting, and teasing us, and we wonder why. When one of the demonic angels grabs us, sometimes we are able to squirm and writhe our way to freedom, but at other times, we become swallowed up by adversaries of God and of good. Either way, we wrestle, but it's hard not to wonder why there has to be so much wrestling in the first place.

We wrestle with the fact that black lives do not seem to matter, and we wonder why God doesn't show up and dismantle white supremacy at its roots.

Justice is possible, but only after wrestling.

Life trains us for the spiritual wrestling we must do in order to improve our own health and the health of the world around us. Life knocks us about the ring until it gets on top of us and pins us down, hindering our movement. So much of the effort of wrestling is working to regain leverage to get back on top. Our opponent—injustice—is not afraid of or intimidated by God. It keeps rolling about, flexing its muscles, seeking to reverse the position and regain control.

We cannot give in to despair. We must remain focused. When we are on the bottom, we have to keep our hips on the mat, our knees bent, and the soles of our feet on the floor so we can push injustice away and regain leverage.

Because life is a wrestling match, the quest for justice will never be a static one. We will always have to wrestle against the powers and principalities. Our goal is to pin our opponent. That means we have to get one or both of injustice's shoulders onto the mat and keep them there for two seconds. When we pin the opponent, we have won this one match, but it is a win nonetheless.

When we wrestle with God, we do so for answers, and if we allow the match to go on long enough, God will win. *We must remain in the match until we get our answer.* We may walk away with a limp, but we will walk away stronger and with clearer spiritual vision. As God is victorious, so are we. Wrestling with God teaches us the technique for wrestling with the demonic angels who seek to defeat us. The bruises and sore joints we get by wrestling with God will strengthen us to wrestle the forces of evil until they submit.

Jacob said to the angel, *"I will not let you go, unless you bless me."*

Neither will we let go or submit. We will wrestle with God so that we can wrestle with injustice and bring it down. We will not let God go unless and until God blesses us.

Amen and amen.

DAY 54

OPPRESSED BY "A HANDFUL OF DYING MEN"

Their delight is in the law of the LORD, and on his law they meditate day and night. They are like trees planted by streams of water, which

yield their fruit in its season, and their leaves do not wither. In all that
they do, they prosper. The wicked are not so, but are like chaff that the
wind drives away.
—Psalm 1:2–4

In his book, *God of the Oppressed*, the late Rev. Dr. James Cone quotes Bishop Daniel Payne of the AME Church, who, in 1852, wrote,

> I began to question the existence of the Almighty, and to say, if indeed there is a God, does he deal justly? Is he a just God? Is he a holy Being? If so, why does he permit a handful of dying men thus to oppress us?[25]

The bishop, like so many African Americans in his time and now, could not understand or reconcile the notion of a good God with the continued presence of, and, indeed, the increase of, race-based oppression. There was too much suffering caused and perpetrated by this "handful of dying men," Payne's reference to the white power structure that, though its members claimed to love the same God as did Payne and other black people, continued to be the gourd from which the politics and policies of oppression were poured.

It is no secret that suffering is everywhere. People all over the world die from earthquakes, tsunamis, tornadoes, hurricanes, and outbreaks of disease. Whenever there is great suffering, people seek to understand why these things occur and they attempt to draw some sense of peace and assurance from God.

We begrudgingly accept the suffering that comes from natural disasters, but the suffering that occurs as a result of hatred and bigotry based on race, gender, sexuality, or even economic status

25. James H. Cone, *God of the Oppressed* (Maryknoll, NY: Orbis Books, 1975), 173.

brings about a different set of emotions and questions. God, who is said to be our *"very present help in trouble"* (Psalm 46:1), has disappointed many of us, allowing this handful of dying men to run roughshod over the rights, dignity, and spirits of far too many people, and we don't understand why.

It begs credulity to understand why the "handful" have claimed so much power and use it to oppress others, in spite of the presence of God. Dr. Cone cites another African American preacher, Nathaniel Paul, who wrote,

> Tell me, ye mighty waters, why did ye sustain the ponderous load of misery?... Oh thou immaculate God, be not angry with us while we come into this thy sanctuary, and make the bold inquiry in this thy holy temple, why it was that thou didst look on with the calm indifference of an unconcerned spectator...?[26]

In our day, a "handful of dying men" pander to the masses by speaking God's name as they continue to wreak havoc, not only in this country but throughout the world. They seem to have a disdain for everyone and everything, except for money and power and the acquisition of both by any means necessary. They gleefully enact laws and policies that cause more and more suffering for those who have already suffered for far too long. The handful are incapable of having the empathy that would help them understand how the masses feel. In truth, the feelings and struggles of the masses are not their concern. Their goal is to keep the power they believe is rightfully—and divinely—theirs.

Many of those who suffer are angry, frustrated, disappointed, and disenchanted, and, in truth, they would prefer not to hear

26. Ibid., 174.

a word about God, the "unconcerned spectator," according to Nathaniel Paul.

But at the end of the day, belief in the presence of God is the only thing that will save the masses from falling into complete despair. Those who suffer have a special relationship with God—even as they question God—that "the handful" does not enjoy. It is that intimacy that keeps the heads of the masses above water and their feet touching bottom. With each and every indignity suffered, they become even more bound and determined not to let the ploys of "the handful" overtake or defeat them.

It is exhausting to always be on one battlefield or another, but our belief in God keeps the world going and is greater than the evil that wants to take us out.

God, who, according to Cone, is "the oppressed One in Jesus," knows what is going on and is ever present to sustain us. If we continue to look for God and reach for God, we will be like trees planted by streams of water, trees that "the handful" will never be able to uproot and destroy.

Amen and amen.

DAY 55
KEEPING VIGIL

Discipline yourselves, keep alert. Like a roaring lion your adversary the devil prowls around, looking for someone to devour.
—1 Peter 5:8

Some years ago, my then-husband and I were traveling to California from Michigan. He was going to begin a residency and I was excited for what lay before us.

We were driving on Interstate 80 in Nebraska when the car started making funny noises. We had it checked out by a local mechanic, who said it would have to be towed some fifty miles back up the highway in order to be fixed, but by that time, everything would be closed. We were told that we could go across the road to get a meal and a room for the night before being towed in the morning.

Unaware of any danger, we went across the road and into a café-type establishment, complete with a pool table lit by a single exposed light bulb. There was another African American couple in the restaurant who had also experienced car trouble. We were glad to see them because everyone else was white and not very friendly looking. We all ate our dinner and then the four of us went to the motel next door to get a room together for the night.

Staying together must have been a message from God because as dusk began to descend, we heard voices outside. Peeking out of the drapes, we saw pickup trucks filled with white men carrying guns. They were laughing and joking and gesturing toward our motel. As it grew darker, more trucks arrived and soon, the trucks were all moving toward the motel and shining their lights into our room. We were terrified. We blocked the door with a barrier of stacked furniture but we knew that if they tried to get in our room, we had nowhere to go.

Nobody slept.

The men (my husband and the other guy) took turns sitting in a chair facing the door, keeping watch. The intimidation continued throughout the night, the white men brandishing long guns and laughing as they taunted us.

We could do nothing but remain vigilant.

As soon as light began to dawn, the pickup trucks left. We were relieved to have survived the night, but we remained ever more cautious for the rest of the trip.

Sometimes, we have to keep vigil to protect ourselves from the powers and principalities that threaten to destroy our lives. There is a true story about an eleven-year-old African American boy who kept vigil in 1904 when his great-grandfather was accosted by white men with guns. They were angry because this poor black man had dared to challenge rich white men who wished to take a mule the black man had paid for. The white men entered the black man's house at night and were about to shoot him, but they hadn't checked the rest of the house and therefore didn't see the little boy who kept vigil nightly with his great-grandfather. As the white men bound and beat the boy's great-grandfather, the boy came out of hiding and shot them. One died. The boy and his family fled the South and settled in Chicago. They were able to survive only because the young boy had kept vigil.

We must also keep vigil and watch for the lies, narratives, and attacks that exist to demoralize us and steal our will to live. Unfortunately, in spite of the presence and power of Jesus, there are forces of evil that wish to see us crumble and fall under the constant pressure. If we are not careful, we can become deeply overwhelmed by the constant trauma we endure that our spirits will collapse and we will consider surrendering the greatest gift God has given us—our very life. We must never allow ourselves to begin down the road of surrender. Our spirits contain the capacity to fight, to believe, to hope, to dream, to get up, to stand up, to survive, and even to thrive—no matter what. Those of us who stand vigil to ward off the invading forces of evil have passed the tests that lead to *testi*monies. It is when we have stood vigil and prevailed that we get a deeper sense of who God is and how good God is, in spite of the evil around us.

On this day, even as so many mourn the recent loss of a civil rights icon, Rev. Dr. James Cone, we must remember how he kept vigil against the forces lined up against him. He kept on working, writing, and teaching people of color and all who are oppressed how to traverse life's dark nights when evil taunts us and dares us to challenge it. In keeping vigil, we might suffer some, but when dawn comes, we will still be standing, moving, and rejoicing that evil did not win. Keeping vigil will help us live the words to the song, "I Still Have Joy":

> After all, after all,
> After everything I've seen,
> Thank God, I still, still, still have joy![27]

The joy is the blessed assurance of God in us, no matter what.

Amen and amen.

DAY 56
WHEN WE LET GOD IN

When you search for me, you will find me; if you seek me with all your heart, I will let you find me, says the LORD, and I will restore your fortunes and gather you from all the nations and all the places where I have driven you, says the LORD, and I will bring you back to the place from which I sent you into exile.
—Jeremiah 29:13–14

---

27. Joseph Pace and the Colorado Mass Choir, "I Still Have Joy," (Integrity Gospel, 2006).

From a very early age, I was moved by the words found in Jeremiah 29:13. For some reason, the words stuck to my very spirit, though I didn't know why. Honestly, I am only just now beginning to understand their depth and power.

Though many of us say we *know* the Lord, it is likely more accurate that we know *about* the Lord, lessons learned from hearing sermons or listening to faithful elders. We may talk a good game, but when push comes to shove, many of us put our own desires before God, we use God for our own gain, and we do not invest the time and effort to have a genuine, intimate relationship with God.

We do not fully let God in.

Howard Thurman revealed what happens when we really let God in. We invite God to peer into our spiritual nakedness. Thurman reminded us that Psalm 139:3 says, *"You search out my path and my lying down, and are acquainted with all my ways."*

> With all my ways Thou art acquainted...the little malices; the big hostilities; the subtle envies; the robust greeds; the whimpering contrition; the great confession; the single resolve; the fearful commitment; the tryst with Death that broods over the zest for life like intermittent shadows from sunrise to sunset.[28]

God is, in fact, well acquainted with all our ways, but until we let God in, we cannot benefit from God's knowledge or from how God can repair our broken places because of that knowledge.

Letting God in requires us to search for God, intentionally, not just in bad times but during the very best times of our lives as well. The promise is that if we search in that way, God *will let us find*

28. Howard Thurman, *For the Inward Journey: The Writings of Howard Thurman* (Richmond, IN: Friends United Meeting, 1991), 102.

Her. And when we find God, weary from a life in which we have marginalized and peripheralized God, we are led into God's divine classroom, where God tells us about ourselves.

In that classroom, God gives us divine treatment. God's treatment is tender yet intentional and robust; God takes divine fingers and unties all of the ropes we have used to bind ourselves together.

It is God's intent that we become free from the shackles of self-deceit. When we let God in, having looked for God with all our heart, God knows that it is okay to begin the process of divine examination, diagnosis, and treatment. God makes sure that our spirits are correctly prepped for the procedure we will undergo. God rejoices in the fact that we sought God, and that we decided to trust God enough to endure this holy procedure.

One of the benefits of letting God in and submitting in ways we may never have done before is that we receive revelations. In some recent meditations I had with God, God reviewed some of the pages and experiences of my life, and then, from nowhere, I heard God say, "You have never cherished yourself."

There is a lot to that revelation but suffice it to say that I *knew* what God was saying as soon as I heard those words. Here I am, "old as Jesus," as I like to say, and even now, God cares enough to give me that piece of hard truth. Those are the kinds of gems we are given when we let God in. What has that truth meant in my life? Once the revelation is given, the work can begin.

God reads us to ourselves; God takes off the cover to reveal all we have hidden so well and so effectively for years, and when we see it, when our eyes have adjusted to the brightness of that moment, we begin to experience spiritual freedom and strength in ways we never imagined possible.

Honestly, I never paid much attention to verse 14 in the text from Jeremiah, the words that say, *"I will let you find me,"* but they make sense. We honor God by our sincere searching, and when God knows we are really serious, God permits us the experience of what it is like to really let God in.

Amen and amen.

DAY 57
ANGER AND CLOGGED EARS

A fool gives full vent to anger, but the wise quietly holds it back.
—Proverbs 29:11

My mother was the most influential theologian in my life before I ever went to seminary. She was fastidious about teaching us what Jesus said and what Jesus meant. She never studied theologians like Paul Tillich, but she knew that sin wasn't just about wearing tight dresses and living "fast" lives, as she had been taught growing up in her "sanctified" church. "Sin," she would say, "is what makes you move away from God, and from Jesus. Whenever you do something that clogs your ears so you can't hear Jesus talking to you, you are sinning."

Sin. That which separates us from God. That was Paul Tillich, but it was also Mary Lee, my mother.

One of the biggest sins, she would say, is anger. "Anger makes you act a fool, and God doesn't like it when anyone acts a fool. That stuff we say and do when we're mad—that's not from God. You can't be holy and be mad all the time."

She always insisted that we practice dealing with anger. We *had* to say we were sorry to each other when we got into fights. We had to say "I love you" to each other, even when we were the most angry. And she stressed that we were not allowed to go to bed angry at each other. "That's what the Bible says," she insisted. "You don't want to go to bed mad at me or Daddy or with each other. You might not make it through the night, and then what? You would die with something clogging your ears and you wouldn't be able to hear Jesus talking to you at the moment you need Him most."

Those were our theology lessons. We all got them. We knew "the gospel according to Mary Lee," and though we have had our struggles, nonetheless, as siblings, we have always had Mary Lee's words to remind us about the danger of anything—including anger—clogging our ears.

I thought about my mother's words recently when I missed my flight to attend the Chautauqua Institution in New York. My flight from Columbus, Ohio, to Philadelphia was an hour late. When we landed, I ran to catch my connecting flight but the door had just closed. I asked if they could let me on, since they had only just closed it, but they said no.

By this time, all of the bags were on board. The fuel hose was taken out of the plane, the jet way was rolled back, and the door was closed. Then the jet sat on the tarmac for a good ten minutes as I stood there watching it. When it finally pushed back, the gate supervisor came in. She didn't look at me or say a word. She stared at her computer as her fingers clattered deftly over the keys, indicating that she had important work to do. Her attitude and spirit spoke loudly: I could just wait.

I was so angry, it felt like my carotid artery would burst. As she stood by her computer station, the desk phone rang. Someone was giving her a hard time. It turns out that she had shut the gate too soon. There were a slew of passengers from another flight who had arrived late and were supposed to be on this same flight. We were all sent to customer service to make other arrangements.

I ended up being stranded in Philadelphia all night. Every time I thought of that young woman (she looked to be no more than thirty years old), I got angry all over again. After being booked on another flight, I went back to the woman and told her that she had been rude to me. She just smirked, which made me even angrier. But just as I was getting ready to power-up on her, I heard Mary Lee's words: "Whenever you do something that clogs your ears so you can't hear Jesus talking to you, you are sinning."

At the time, I didn't care much about whether or not I was sinning but I should have. Since sin is anything that separates us from God, it is something we need to avoid at all costs, for our own sakes! The sin of anger is debilitating; it steals our joy and our capacity to be rational and fair, and it urges us to say things we ought not to say—words we cannot take back. Anger messes with our blood pressure and our entire physiology. Anger—the sin—can kill us or at least make us seriously ill.

It took me much of the day to clean the anger from my pores. Mary Lee was right; anger was clogging my ears so that all I could hear was my own ranting. I had pushed God to the periphery of my soul. We have to deal with anger so it does not get between us and God. Anger cannot be allowed to control us. Too often, it does.

I didn't go to bed angry at the young woman in the airport because I didn't go to bed, period. The last flight of the evening was canceled after having been delayed several times. The first flight out the next morning was so ridiculously early that I would have had to return to the airport almost as soon as I would have arrived at a hotel. Yes, I was angry much of the day, but as I wrestled with that anger, I was grateful to experience a moment of revelation; God had turned my mourning into a dance of reflection and prayer.

Mary Lee's words remind us that when we are angry, the best thing is to seek God and to be earnest about it. The prophet Jeremiah wrote, *"When you search for me, you will find me; if you seek me with all your heart"* (Jeremiah 29:13). If we can give our whole heart to God, as opposed to squatting in our own anger, even if that process takes a while, we will close the chasm we create between us and God.

Amen and amen.

DAY 58
FACING WHAT WE MUST

A fool gives full vent to anger, but the wise quietly holds it back.
—Proverbs 29:11

There are things we do not care to see or acknowledge, as if not seeing or acknowledging them will make them go away. A mother once shared that she wondered if her daughter was doing drugs but she was afraid to ask. Another person said that he had been feeling bad for a while but chalked it up to being tired. He ended up in a hospital for triple-bypass surgery.

We do not want to face things that seem too big for us to handle or are too painful for us to consider because we just do not want to deal with it.

What I have learned is that not facing something does not make it go away. Putting ourselves in a zone of denial does not result in a pleasant outcome. Some of us do not want to acknowledge that we are getting old, some do not want to acknowledge that the cough or fatigue they've been having seems abnormal. Some of us do not want to acknowledge that a person we love is not giving anything back and may in fact be toxic to our spirits.

The long-term effect of denial is a deep spiritual pain that we bring upon ourselves. Facing what we must may be painful initially but, in the long run, it is liberating to face adversity and all its consequences…and move on.

Iyanla Vanzant shared a poem that her now-deceased daughter, Gemmia, once wrote. She used the title of the poem for one of her first books: *One Day My Soul Just Opened Up*. It can mean a lot of things to a lot of people, but for those of us who refuse to face the things we must, it has a strong message. It reads:

> One day my soul just opened up
> And things started happenin'
> Things I can't quite explain,
> I mean,
> I cried and cried like never before
> I cried tears of ten thousand mothers
> I couldn't even feel anything because
> I cried til I was numb.
>
> One day my soul just opened up
> I felt this overwhelming pride
> What I was proud of
> Only God knows!
> Like the pride of a hundred thousand fathers
> Basking in the glory of their newborn sons
> I was grinnin' from ear to ear!

One day my soul just opened up
I started laughing
And I laughed for what seemed like forever
Wasn't nothin' particularly funny goin' on
But I laughed anyhow
I laughed the joy of a million children playin'
In the mud
I laughed 'til my sides ached
Oh, God! It felt so good!

One day my soul just opened up
There were revelations, annihilations, and resolutions
Feelings of doubt and betrayal, vengeance and forgiveness
Memories of things I'd seen and done before
Of places I'd been, although I didn't know when
There were lives I'd lived
People I'd loved
Battles I'd fought
Victories I'd won
And wars I'd lost.

One day, my soul just opened up
And out poured all the things
I'd been hiding
And denying
And living through
That had just happened moments before.

One day, my soul just opened up
And I decided
I was good and ready!
Good and ready!
To surrender

My life
To God.

So, with my soul wide open,
I sat down
Wrote her a note
And told her so.[29]

If we face what we must, our souls might open as well, and only God knows how our lives will bend toward the presence of the God, who desires that we thrive in this life and not walk blindly.

Give your spirit the opportunity to be truly free.

Amen and amen.

DAY 59
WHAT'S YOU NAME?

Truly I tell you, just as you did it to one of the least of these who are members of my family, you did it to me.
—Matthew 25:40

During the 1960s, many white churches in both the North and the South opposed integration. Many of them adopted "whites-only" membership policies, refusing to admit that their attitudes contradicted Scripture or the will of God. In fact, many churches taught that those who fought *for* the civil rights of black people were putting their own salvation in jeopardy.

There were a courageous few members of the clergy who disagreed with racial discrimination and said so, but only a few.

29. Iyanla Vanzant, *One Day My Soul Just Opened Up* (New York: Atria Books, 1998).

One such white man was Sam Ashmore, editor of the *Mississippi Methodist Advocate*. Responding to the racial showdown between Alabama Governor George Wallace and African American students who, according to court order, were attempting to enter the University of Mississippi, Ashmore said, "Yes, the church is partly responsible for what happened at Ole Miss. Because we were not more vocal and outspoken; because we were not true to our Christian Convictions, we aided anarchy."[30] Another white pastor, Rev. Charles Stanford Jr., said, "Those of us who have remained silent on a great and grave moral issue have lent support to those who have spoken out on the side of error and evil."[31]

Racism is just as virulent today. Almost all of our social ills—mass incarceration, systemic poverty, unemployment, drug traffic, crime—can be traced to a racist core. But there is yet another issue of discrimination that is growing more and more rampant today: discrimination against the LGBTQ community.

A mother came crying to me the other day. Her eleven-year-old daughter believed herself to be a boy. She was beside herself. "What should I do?" she asked. Where should she turn? This African American Christian woman already bore the burden of constant discrimination. Now this.

Most people today would rather not deal with the complex issues of sexual identity. It's much easier to just remain silent.

I believe Jesus calls us to advocate for any and all of *"the least of these"* (Matthew 25:40), and not just for those with whom we closely identify. It is a risk to advocate for others; I believe it's called "the cost of discipleship."

---

30. Carolyn Renee Dupont, *Mississippi Prayer: Southern White Evangelicals and the Civil Rights Movement, 1945–1975* (New York: NYU Press, 2013), 143.
31. Ibid.

When my son Charlie was still little enough to wear those one-piece, seersucker jumpsuits, I took him with our church on a bowling outing. Charlie was fascinated with the heavy balls and the crashing sounds, the shiny bowling lanes and those tipsy pins. His eyes were wide as saucers. I left him with church members as I got everyone checked in. When I returned, Charlie was standing in the middle of a bowling lane, hands behind his back, looking at the group of church people. Someone had called for him to come back, but Charlie, unmoved, said, "What's YOU name?"

He wasn't going to come to just anyone.

I think of that day when I think of Jesus calling us. I think of Jesus asking, "What's YOU name? Is My work safe in your hands? Do you have the strength to stand up for 'the least of these,' those who are being pushed down? Will you do it, whatever the cost? Is My Word safe with you?"

The way we answer that question might well depend on who we understand Jesus to be. Jesus asked His disciples who they thought He was. They replied, *"Some say John the Baptist, but others Elijah, and still others Jeremiah or one of the prophets"* (Matthew 16:14).

Jesus pressed in and asked, *"But who do you say that I am?"* (verse 15).

Simon Peter said, *"You are the Messiah, the Son of the living God"* (verse 16).

As during slavery, too many Christians seem complacent with, even disconnected from, a suffering world. Perhaps it is a symptom of how rugged American individualism has infected our Christianity, giving us a personal Savior but little empathy for those He came to save. But Jesus was concerned for far more than the redemption of individuals—He wanted to redeem the very powers that shape the dominations system in which we live. To do that, He is going to need an army of people who know who Jesus the Christ is and what He is about, and people who know who they are in Him. Jesus asks us who we say *He* is. Then He asks who *we* are. Only then, it seems, can He determine if we are fit for the call to do God's work.

"What's YOU name?"

Amen. And amen.

DAY 60
WHEN WE SILENCE GOD

O LORD, you have searched me and known me. You know when I sit down and when I rise up; you discern my thoughts from far away. You search out my path and my lying down, and are acquainted with all my ways…. Where can I go from your spirit? Or where can I flee from your presence? If I ascend to heaven, you are there; if I make my bed in Sheol, you are there. If I take the wings of the morning and settle at the farthest limits of the sea, even there your hand shall lead me, and your right hand shall hold me fast.
—Psalm 139:1–3, 7–10

It hardly seems possible that we, who cry out for God in our moments of pain and confusion, can silence God.

The late Rabbi Abraham Heschel, who walked with Dr. King during the civil rights movement, taught that instead of us asking where our ever-present God is, we ought to consider that God is asking where *we* are. He wrote, "We live in an age when most of us have ceased to be shocked by the increasing breakdown in moral inhibitions. The decay of conscience fills the air with a pungent smell. Good and evil, which were once as distinguishable as day and night, have become a blurred mist. But that mist is man-made. God is not silent. He has been silenced."[32]

The erosion of moral inhibitions causing horrific events like the slave trade and the Holocaust, mass incarceration, and extreme poverty, is evidence that God has been expelled from our day-to-day lives, in spite of our pious declarations that we love God. God was expelled from the garden of Eden though God never left Adam and Eve; *they abandoned God.*

When we push God out, God obliges; God withdraws from us, said Heschel, leaving us to ourselves. And we, left to ourselves, act like teenagers, unwilling to be told anything, rejecting direction and authority, even from God. Some of us assume that God must be near but we minimize the value of that assurance. Heschel said, "We have trifled with the name of God. We have taken ideals in vain, preached and eluded Him, praised and defied Him. Now we reap the fruits of failure."[33]

Despite God's exile, God beckons. God begs to be readmitted into our spirits. We do ourselves a great disservice by shutting God out.

I have shut God out. There have been times when I should have been on my face, praying to God but I chose not to. I can remember feeling a divine *pull*. Instinctively, I knew it was God, beckoning me to enter into a conversation with Her instead of depending on my own consciousness or other people. And yet, I resisted. In the midst of my struggles, I have cried out, "God, where are You?" And all the time, God was working, often unsuccessfully, to connect with me.

In spite of our tendency to silence God, God remains. God searches us and knows us, even when we push God out of our lives.

32. Abraham Joshua Heschel, *Man Is Not Alone: A Philosophy of Religion* (New York: Farrar, Straus and Giroux, 1951), 152.
33. Ibid.

God extends a hand when we feel weary and burdened. When we refuse to take the hand, God withdraws, but God never leaves us.

How absolutely gracious is our God, who stands by and waits for an invitation to enter into our souls. How amazing is the love of this God, who does not turn permanently against us because of our ignorance and lack of gratitude. What must God want to say to us right now, want us to hear, so that our lives and our society may become better?

When I first heard that we can silence God, I was stunned, but the revelation is timely. In these days, when there is so much uncertainty due to what is going on in our country, we cannot afford to push God into exile. The chaos that swirls around us and seems destined to cause great destruction begs us to reexamine our relationship with God to see if we have silenced God. If so, we must move to correct that situation immediately. God is near; God's hand is outstretched; God's presence is what we need in order to handle the vicissitudes of life.

Lord, in Your mercy, hear our prayer.

Amen and amen.

DAY 61
WHEN WORDS ARE EMPTY

Blessed be the God and Father of our Lord Jesus Christ, the Father of mercies and the God of all consolation, who consoles us in all our affliction, so that we may be able to console those who are in any affliction with the consolation with which we ourselves are consoled by God.
—2 Corinthians 1:3-4

In the aftermath of a mass shooting, we hear the same words, again and again: "Our thoughts and prayers are with you."

They have been uttered so often they begin to sound empty. What do they mean? What are "thoughts and prayers"?

The words sound empty because the attitudes in this nation are not likely to change when it comes to guns. Dietrich Bonhoeffer wrote, "We have succumbed to secularism.... Not godlessness or cultural Bolshevism at all, but the *Christian* renunciation of God as the Lord of the Earth." He later concluded, "This pious secularism also makes it possible to preach and say nice things."[34]

Christians are good at saying nice things.

But empty words can cut a person to the core. If we say "I love you" without meaning it, the recipient of those words feels our lack of investment and truth, and suffers emotional turmoil. If we say, "I'm sorry," but keep doing the same thing, over and over, we breed a spirit of anger and cynicism in the one to whom we are apologizing. If we say, "I promise to be there," but fail to show up, our words only serve to agitate instead of soothe.

People resort to "pious secularism" in times of great national tragedy because it feels like the only appropriate thing to do. But to hear the words over and over, when there is no intention of ever changing the instigating behavior, makes them seem like easy and empty platitudes.

Empty words do more harm than good. They are more of a slap in the face than a source of comfort. Insincere "thoughts and prayers" are not enough. In a time of great pain, people need genuine

---

34. Dietrich Bonhoeffer, *Berlin: 1932–1933: Dietrich Bonhoeffer Works, Volume 12* (Minneapolis, MN: Augsburg Fortress Press, 2009), 287.

empathy and care. When any relationship is troubled, it needs honesty and truth so that there can be reconciliation and resolution.

Empty words cause us to feel the pain even more. When suffering, we look for comfort. The psalmist wrote, *"As a deer longs for flowing streams, so my soul longs for you, O God"* (Psalm 42:1). In that yearning for God, empty words do not suffice.

Amen and amen.

DAY 62
TO BE A COFFEE BEAN

Jesus told his disciples, "If any want to become my followers, let them deny themselves and take up their cross and follow me. For those who want to save their life will lose it, and those who lose their life for my sake will find it. For what will it profit them if they gain the whole world but forfeit their life?"
—Matthew 16:24–26

I once heard a presentation by a young man who had taken some wrong turns in life and was given what was, essentially, a lifelong prison sentence.

In prison, an older inmate told him a story. Prison, the man said, is like a pot of hot water, and it is up to you to decide what you will be as you serve your time. You can be a carrot, an egg, or a coffee bean. The older man posed a question: "What happens when you throw a carrot into hot water?" The young man said, "It gets soft." "Correct," replied the older man. "In here you don't want to be a carrot. If guys see you are soft, you will not do well."

The older inmate posed another question: "What happens when you put an egg into hot water?" "It gets hard," replied the young man. "Correct again," the older man said. "In here you don't want to get hard. You'll become like the gangs, hardened by hatred and anger."

Then the older man asked, "What happens when you put a coffee bean into hot water?" The young man answered, "The water turns brown." "Yes," the older man said. "The coffee bean changes the water. That's what you want to do. You want to change your environment for the better. You want to be a coffee bean."

The story was simple, but powerful and transformative. For the new inmate, it became a part of his own personal mantra: "I want to be a coffee bean." With that thought, he turned from an addict into a new man, wanting to get out of prison so he could help other young people avoid the mistakes he had made. He turned to God in ways he had never done before and was released from prison after serving only seven years.

The story caused me to pause.

Who of us can say that we want to be agents of change in this world? It is far more comfortable to become a hardboiled egg. Hardened within and without, we shield ourselves from all that is uncomfortable and displeasing. We shield ourselves from communication with difficult people. We turn our eyes away from the degradation around us and refuse to see our own complicity in it. We claim to be too busy to hear others' cries for help.

It is easier that way. Less hassle.

But to be a coffee bean is to be a companion of God. It indicates a willingness to lose ourselves for something greater than ourselves. It is to be willing to deny ourselves and "take up our crosses" in order to confront elements of this life that negatively affect others. We must impact our environment by becoming a voice for the voiceless and the downtrodden in this world.

When you do, you will notice how it affects others. People respond to coffee beans.

The world around us is hot water, begging for people to become coffee beans and bring justice, peace, and love into the world. The world is yearning for change; we are the way for change to happen.

Since I heard that young man's presentation, I have never looked at coffee beans in quite the same way. Nor have I looked at hard-boiled eggs or carrots the same way. Being too soft or too hard is not the way any of us should live. At the end of the day, we should all have coffee-bean stories to tell. In doing so, we can testify and affirm that leaving your comfort zone and standing up for change works. It will attract and inspire others to be the change they desire to see.

Amen and amen.

DAY 63
TRYING TO COMPREHEND THE INCOMPREHENSIBLE

Why, O Lord, do you stand far off? Why do you hide yourself in times of trouble? In arrogance the wicked persecute the poor—let them be caught in the schemes they have devised. …Rise up, O Lord; O God, lift up your hand; do not forget the oppressed. Why do the wicked renounce God, and say in their hearts, "You will not call us to account"? But you do see! Indeed you note trouble and grief, that you may take it into your hands; the helpless commit themselves to you; you have been the helper of the orphan.
—Psalm 10:1-2, 12–14

It is said that the Rev. Dr. Martin Luther King Jr. always carried a copy of Howard Thurman's book *Jesus and the Disinherited*. Thurman was greatly influenced by Mahatma Gandhi, who, during a 1935 trip to India, told Thurman that "it may be through the Negroes that the unadulterated message of nonviolence will be delivered to the world."[35]

Dr. Thurman influenced King greatly as dean of the Chapel at Boston University when King was a student there. Some years later, after Dr. King had been stabbed during a book signing, Dr. Thurman told the emerging civil rights leader to use this unexpected tragedy as an opportunity to stop and meditate on his life and his purpose. It was advice that was life-transforming.

Thurman advised King to extend his healing period by two weeks. It would give him time away from the pressures and issues of the movement. "Thurman worried that 'the movement had become more than an organization; it had become an organism with a life of its own,' which potentially could swallow up King."[36] Dr. King took the advice. He studied Thurman's scholarly and theological views and gleaned a concept of Jesus the Christ that profoundly affected his future work and writings.

According to Thurman, understanding Jesus as a social activist, human and yet divine, who believed in the inherent worth of all people, is life-giving and easier to comprehend than the commonly communicated image of the Father or Parent of Jesus—God. God's ways often do not seem fair or just. It is hard, sometimes, to put the words "good" and "God" together, because so much in our

35. Paul Harvey, "This Theologian Helped MLK See the Value of Nonviolence," Smithsonianmag.com, January 12, 2008 (https://www.smithsonianmag.com/history/this-theologian-helped-mlk-see-value-nonviolence-180967821/#1Tfue56chMD1uqbl.99, accessed July 20, 2019.)
36. Ibid.

lives is not, in fact, good at all. The incomprehensible is a relentless presence in our lives. It tempts us to question God, something our parents and grandparents taught us we should never do.

Yet, without questions, we will never move beyond the incomprehensible in front of us. We cannot understand why God seems silent and permissive in the face of persistent racism, sexism, homophobia, and xenophobia. We struggle with doubts and questions that grate against the advice and warnings of our elders, who taught us to hold our tongues and accept the fact that God is good, all the time.

The psalmists, however, made room for the doubters to publicly wrestle with God. They aired their struggles for all to see. In doing so, they allow space for us to admit our hurt and the freedom to shout our displeasure. The doubters are made more powerful through their questions to God because, in questioning, their relationship with God becomes more life-giving and sustaining.

Thurman and King both questioned and wrestled with God, getting enough answers to show us a pathway through the darkness to the Spirit of God. And in that seeking, we are armed with God's own Spirit, a powerful force that is mightier than any gun, hateful epithet, or oppressive social system. The presence of God's Spirit within us is a gift and as an old hymn states, "the world didn't give it and the world can't take it away."

Many of us are at risk of being swallowed up by the resistance work we are doing. Perhaps we are at risk of being swallowed up by our own anger, frustration, fear, or emotional angst. Perhaps we, too, need to heed Dr. Thurman's advice to stop and wrestle with and meditate on our life and our purpose. Our souls need healing in order to be made whole; only whole spirits can approach the incomprehensible with a measure of peace despite our unanswered questions about God. With that peace comes power to withstand the fires of life. Soon, the incomprehensible diminishes in our sight, and we are able to move forward.

And in the end, that is what God would have us do. It is the way God helps us to overcome the incomprehensible.

Amen and amen.

DAY 64

WHEN THE SUN'S RAYS ARE WEAKEST

In the heavens he has set a tent for the sun, which comes out like a bridegroom from his wedding canopy, and like a strong man runs its course with joy. Its rising is from the end of the heavens, and its circuit to the end of them; and nothing is hid from its heat.
—Psalm 19:4–6

I love walking my dog in the cool of the morning. Even during a hot summer month, at dawn, the coolness of the night before still hovers over everything. Soon, the sun moves higher and the air grows warmer. The sun and earth work in relationship with each other; it is the earth's relationship with the sun that accounts for the temperatures we experience. The dark side of the earth is experiencing the weakest rays of the sun and loses heat during the night as it radiates heat into the atmosphere. It is not until the sun's rays come back into direct contact with the earth's surface that this process is reversed and things begin to get hot again.

I find it intriguing that something as powerful as the sun could become weak at any time. But the sun's heat is weakest on the dark side of the earth right before dawn as the sun reemerges and fights to regain supremacy.

If the sun's rays can be weakened, we should not be surprised or troubled when we, at times, find ourselves weakening. Everyone is weak at one time or another. We all have natural cycles of dawn and dusk in which our power becomes diminished. We have all been through a "night," in which our confidence, our hope, and our faith have "radiated out" into the darkness. The spiritual strength we need in order to move and function must compete with our dark "night." And just as dawn comes every morning, a time when the sun's rays reestablish their dominance, we also have dawns in our lives when our spiritual strength fights to regain its rightful place.

Bouts of weakness are nothing to be ashamed of. Especially as we understand how nature works. We are an extension of nature; we can see how God works in us by watching how God works in nature. If even the majesty of God allows for the weakness of the sun's rays right before dawn, we can expect that our sojourn will not be any different.

Night comes in our lives, a time when our vision is impaired and we feel weak. At such times, we need a special kind of strength, a different kind of energy, to keep going. We look for the light—the sun—but even when we see it dawning, we are still fighting the principalities and powers that have rejoiced and participated in our temporary loss of strength.

Our comfort is in knowing that as the sun's rays do not retreat, neither does the intentionality of God. Every day, God comes. Every day, God keeps on being God, bringing us to a place where we can feel the full power of God. Where we have been cold, shivering from our losses, we become strong, warmed by God's presence.

In August 2017, when racial hatred erupted in Charlottesville, Virginia, at a Unite the Right Rally, we were pushed deeper into a cold night that had been coming for a while. As the full fury of what happened in Charlottesville blew up, the night became darker and darker. It is a nighttime familiar to those who had battled white supremacy a generation prior.

It had not gone away. We are still deep in this night. The racist dog whistles and political rallies continue. It feels like it will take some time for the power of God to break through and improve things. There are times when the radiating hate makes the rays of God's presence seem "weak." But just as the power of the sun never diminishes, neither does the radiance of the Spirit of God. We might be troubled, but we need to remember that though dawn may be the coldest part of any day, the warm rays of the sun still prevail.

And God's warmth will prevail.

Amen and amen.

DAY 65
KILLING OUR MOCKINGBIRDS

My brothers and sisters, do you with your acts of favoritism really believe in our glorious Lord Jesus Christ? For if a person with gold rings and in fine clothes comes into your assembly, and if a poor person in dirty clothes also comes in, and if you take notice of the one wearing the fine clothes and say, "Have a seat here, please," while to the one who is poor you say, "Stand there," or, "Sit at my feet," have you not made distinctions among yourselves, and become judges with evil thoughts?
—James 2:1–4

In Harper Lee's classic, *To Kill a Mockingbird*, Atticus Finch reminds his daughter Scout that it is a sin to kill a mockingbird. Scout is confused and asks their neighbor, Miss Maudie, what it means. Miss Maudie replies, "Mockingbirds don't do one thing but make music for us to enjoy. They don't eat up people's gardens, don't nest in corncribs, they don't do one thing but sing their hearts out for us. That's why it's a sin to kill a mockingbird."[37]

The metaphor references anyone wanting to hurt Boo Radley, an eccentric neighborhood outcast. Later in the book, it applies to Tom Robinson, a black man accused and convicted of a crime he did not commit. Boo Radley had been damaged by an abusive father. Tom Robinson had been damaged by an abusive, racist system.

I have always loved that quote about mockingbirds. In our lives, we all have mockingbirds, people who only want to make us happy. Too often, we ignore them because they are not the people whom we *want* paying attention to us, or gaining entrance to our inner circle. While they "serve" us with unfettered joy, we reject them, in effect killing their spirit and their love.

Why do we do that? Why do we downplay *anyone* who accepts us for who we are, who do not care about the mistakes we have made or the wrong turns we have taken?

We yearn for that which seems unattainable. We yearn for the status we do not have, for the social circles in which we are not accepted, for the praise of people we think are important, while ignoring the people near us who see us for who we are.

What we do not realize, in our own shortsightedness, is that we are doing to someone else what is being done to us. We do not

---

37. Harper Lee, *To Kill a Mockingbird* (New York: Hachette Book Group USA, 1960), 119.

see the hurt they experience from being rejected and ignored. We cannot appreciate the fact that God put them in our lives to be our mockingbirds. They sing to us in everything they do, but we do not hear. We reject them as we have been rejected.

Often, it is only after we kill the mockingbirds in our lives that we realize how beautiful their music had been. Only when their presence is gone and their voices have been stilled do we realize that we rejected the music of acceptance and love that God put into our lives.

It is a sin to kill the mockingbirds in our lives.

In *To Kill a Mockingbird*, Boo Radley's heart was good; he was a loner and a recluse because of his father's neglect and abuse, but he still had enough love in him to protect Jem and Scout. Tom Robinson was damaged by a racist world but still had enough God in him to stand with dignity despite being mistreated and maligned. All he had ever tried to do was live a good life and provide music in the form of his presence to those whom he loved. His music was not appreciated by this racist world. At the end of his rope, he tried to escape from prison and was shot in the back seventeen times.

The mockingbird was killed, his voice and contributions silenced and terminated.

We silence the mockingbirds in our lives with our rejection. We kill what we love and need most—mockingbirds, put into our lives by God to bring us joy.

Maybe we should stop and try to listen to the mockingbirds around us…and be blessed. They cannot raise your status or bring you wealth and fame. They merely sing for you and love you. It would be an affront to God, it seems, to ignore what God has put in our lives.

Amen and amen.

DAY 66
ON FORGIVENESS AND LOVE

Whoever does not take up the cross and follow me is not worthy of me. Those who find their life will lose it, and those who lose their life for my sake will find it.
—Matthew 10:38–39

Jesus's teachings have often caused me to squirm. He directed us to do things that sometimes feel antithetical to being human. Certainly, forgiving people whom you would rather forget and loving your enemy are two of the most troubling and challenging of all His teachings.

We are prone to criticize and judge each other; we are also prone to holding grudges. It may be that holding grudges makes us feel safer, less vulnerable to attacks from others, but in fact, holding grudges serves as a barrier between us and God. We cannot be in a genuine relationship with God if we are not in relationship with God's children—all of God's children.

If we value our lives with Jesus the Christ, we don't have the luxury of ignoring the things Jesus commanded us to do. In Matthew 10:38, Jesus says, "*Whoever does not take up the cross and follow me is not worthy of me.*" Certainly, loving someone who has worked to destroy you, and forgiving that person, amounts to taking up your cross—for it is indeed heavy—but Jesus says that if we do not do it, *we are not worthy* of Him, and of the gift of life that Jesus offers.

In thinking about what is going on in this nation, it becomes clear that if we want the privilege of calling Jesus our Lord, then we must practice forgiveness and love. The blatant in-your-face racism that sprouts around us, with all of its arrogance, is difficult to take.

Forgiving does not mean we condone the things that racists say and do; forgiving simply means we free up enough spiritual and emotional strength to not let their words and actions paralyze us with despair. What would our racist political leaders do if a group of people, unwilling to displease Jesus, would encircle the White House and Capitol and pray for them? Is there a limit to what God can do? And what happens to *us* if we sit in our frustration, anger, and even hatred of such people? Are we willing to remain in our anger and hatred and risk becoming what they are—"unworthy" of a relationship with Jesus the Christ?

Many think it is a sign of weakness to pray for and to love those who want to destroy you. And yet, it was forgiveness and love that Dr. King taught, lessons that he took from the gospel. We are called to hold our leaders accountable, to challenge their policies, and to move past their hateful rhetoric. To decide to love and forgive someone, even as you do everything in your power to oppose and fight what they are doing, is a sign that you understand what taking up your cross is all about.

If we pray while we work, we can be instruments of God's peace.

Maybe this is a time when our actions show even the most bigoted, hateful people that we, too, are children of faith who answer to God and not to humans. Maybe *we* were saved for such a time as this.

Amen and amen.

DAY 67

WHEN YOU KNOW YOU'VE LET GO

Humble yourselves therefore under the mighty hand of God, so that
he may exalt you in due time. Cast all your anxiety on him, because
he cares for you.
—1 Peter 5:6–7

A few weeks ago, I was watching thick maple syrup roll gently over top of the pancakes I had ordered. At the same table sat my daughter, who had ordered waffles. She poured her syrup, too, which pooled in the little squares that make waffles...waffles.

It hit me as I looked the pancakes and the waffles that the way the syrup was falling is the way "stuff" sticks to us. "Stuff" includes sticky substances like anger, hurt, and betrayal. On good days, our pain glides over us and falls down the sides of our spirits; on bad days, the pain gets stuck, like syrup pooled in the little waffle squares. Either way, the "stuff" sticks, and it damages us.

While syrup makes pancakes and waffles taste good, raw, hurtful emotions sour our spirits. While syrup makes pancakes moist and delicious, raw emotions dry us out so we are unable to absorb the good things in our lives.

Richard Rohr says, "Authentic spirituality is always on some level or in some way about *letting go*."[38] Mature spirits are able to let go; immature spirits cannot. Mature spirits are *willing* to let God be God, even when it is not clear how God will make things right. Immature spirits are *willful*, fighting against God in spite of

---

38. Richard Rohr, "Letting Go as a Way of Life," Center for Action and Contemplation, June 7, 2015, https://cac.org/letting-go-way-life-2015-06-07/ (accessed July 21, 2019).

declaring love for God. Our willfulness keeps our pain pooled in the crevices of our spirits, like syrup in waffles.

Dr. Martin Luther King recognized that there was much pain, bitterness, and rage in the souls of black people. He spoke of a two-way flow between pain and anger on one side, and action and resistance on the other. In order to survive, there had to be a way for black people to let go of pain and anger. Part of getting rid of pain was through protesting, singing freedom songs, and defiantly rejecting oppression, despite not knowing what that rejection would mean.

Perhaps it is because we do not know what "letting go" will bring that we hold on to emotions that are not good for us. We cannot predict what God will do. We are not sure that what God does will be timely or something we *desire* God to do. We remain willful because being willing seems too dangerous and makes us feel too vulnerable.

But when we decide to become willing, we gain freedom. As Rohr says, "Freedom is…letting go of our need to control and manipulate God and others. It is even letting go of our need to know and our need to be right—which we only discover with maturity."[39]

When we become willing to trust God, we lose the need to see someone hurt for the way they hurt us. In doing so, we break out of our self-imposed emotional and spiritual prisons and we are finally free.

Our souls open up; we are able to break out of the armor that has kept us bound, and we are free. We no longer worry about what will happen to the person, persons, or situations that brought us pain. We can rejoice that God has brought us through a wilderness

---

39. Ibid.

to the edge of a Sea of Reeds, where we can pass over on dry land to a new world, a new beginning, a new chapter.

We have a choice. We can remain willful or we can ask God to help us become willing to be free. If we do that, the chains will fall off and we will fly, as God always intended us to do.

Amen and amen.

DAY 68

WHEN WE MUST USE ANOTHER PART OF OUR SPIRIT

The mind governed by the flesh is death, but the mind governed by the Spirit is life and peace.
—Romans 8:6 NIV

I was surprised to learn that people who stutter do not stutter when they sing.

In fact, when stutterers are able to slightly sing their words or even use a different type of vocal inflection, they can effectively shut down the stutter. The reason Marilyn Monroe spoke in hushed, whispered tones was not to sound alluring and sexy but an attempt to hide the fact that she was a stutterer. I once heard a woman give a talk in which she stuttered constantly but then sang for five minutes without a single stutter.

The medical reason for this is that human speech is controlled by the left side of the brain, while singing is controlled by the right side of the brain. When we sing, we apparently sing "from the heart," demanding a different skill set than we do when we speak. Of course, it is a lot more complicated than that but, basically, we use a different part of our brains when we sing, a part that pushes aside the activity of the left brain that causes stuttering.

B. B. King, Nancy Wilson, and Carly Simon were all stutterers.

But God is great. The same God who made it possible for a person to sing without stuttering is the same God who can get us to let go of the issues, experiences, memories, and words that have kept our spirits enslaved to spiritual and emotional pain. How can God do that?

Part of the solution is in concentrating on the beauty of God's holiness, the majesty of God's creative genius. When a stutterer sings, he or she relies on the part of the brain that controls the vocal cords, lips, and tongue. Likewise, there is a part of our spirit that controls the way we see, hear, and perceive the world. All around us, God has put things that demand we come out of ourselves and *see* that the Lord is good. Alice Walker wrote about it in *The Color Purple*: "I think it pisses God off if you walk by the color purple in a field somewhere and don't notice it. …People think pleasing God is all God care about. But any fool living in the world can see it always trying to please us back."[40]

Like the stutterer, when we don't access another part of our spirit, we can become twisted up, tightly coiled, mumbling, and unable to move through life with joy and purpose. Surely, God would want us to find the part of our spirit that may yet be unused, the part that has a song dying to be sung. It is worth the effort at least to look for it.

Amen and amen.

---

40. Alice Walker, *The Color Purple* (San Diego, CA: Harcourt, 1982), 196.

DAY 69

THE PATH OF THE FAMILIAR

The thief comes only to steal and kill and destroy. I came that they may have life, and have it abundantly.
—John 10:10

Many years ago, Dr. Martin Luther King referred to the "giant triplets of racism, materialism, and militarism" and declared that they were "strangling the soul of America."[41] A year later, he was gunned down in Memphis, his voice forever stilled.

He was walking a path of the familiar. Racism, materialism, and militarism have been barriers in the quest for justice ever since there have been governments and people. The American empire is not so different from the Roman Empire, or any other empire. The path of the familiar is well-traveled and has stubbornly resisted efforts to be transformed or dismantled.

We, God's people, also traverse the same path, empire after empire. Although many people may regard certain politicians as "the worst ever," in truth, they are not so different from their predecessors. Arrogant and ignorant, brash and egotistical, insecure and weak—we've seen this before.

The path of the familiar.

These paths are found throughout history. We have often walked on them without knowing it. But when we refuse to acknowledge the path, fail to identify an empire for what it is, and continue to go where they lead us, we will not get to where God wants us to be.

---

41. Martin Luther King speech "Beyond Vietnam: A Time to Break Silence," delivered on April 4, 1967, at Riverside Church in New York City.

In our work for justice, there are always at least two paths—the path of the familiar and the path that leads into the unknown. It is scary to go a new way, to blaze a new path, or to do a new thing. It is scary to not be familiar with the ground on which we walk. We do not know what it will cost us to step into an unknown space but if we do not take an unfamiliar path, we will never arrive anywhere new. Walking the same path has imprisoned us, kept us "in our place," and circled us back to where we started.

God wants us to abandon the path of the familiar and risk change, loss, and pain. It is called faith, yes, but also courage. We are afraid to leave what we know—even if we know how bad it is. We are afraid to jump in because of how deep the water might be. But God wants us to leave the path of the familiar behind and blaze new paths. God wants us to go where we never even dreamed of going. Jesus the Christ came so that we might have life and have it abundantly.

The abundance we seek might be found on the unfamiliar paths we are so careful to avoid.

Amen and amen.

DAY 70
THE DEAFENING SILENCE OF LOSS

Blessed are those who mourn, for they will be comforted.
—Matthew 5:4

After we experience the loss of a loved one, we experience a weird silence and a gaping hole. The busy bustling world continues to hum all around us as we are lost in the fog of silence and grief.

The silence only grows deeper by the day. It begins the moment our loved one takes his or her final breath. Our world stops and we grapple with the loss. Within moments, emptiness mixes in with the grief. As we leave the physical presence of our deceased loved one, the silence follows. We can almost hear it. Pain rushes in but it's the silence that makes the pain so much worse than we expected it to be.

The silence doesn't just occur when we suffer personal loss. It also comes when a beloved cultural figure passes. When Dr. Martin Luther King was killed, the silence was there. When Prince, Michael Jackson, and Whitney Houston died, the silence was there. In its persistence, this silence is a roar that reminds us things are not the same.

The silence hurts. It haunts us. When we get into the car, it is there. When we walk into the house, it is there. When we pass places that remind us of our loved one, it is there. It comes up with the dawn and refuses to set with the sun. It can wake us up with a jolt in the middle of the night. It can be so loud in our spirits that it drowns out the voices of those trying to comfort us.

No matter how hard we try, we are unable to get rid of the painful experience of loss. Every single one of us have, and will continue to have, bouts of silence caused by loss.

Loss is a given in life. We cannot live unless we experiences loss. God did not give us a handbook on how to handle it; we do not know how to cope with the silence. We cannot force it into a locked closet or pack it away and send it off. We must learn to live with it. We must know that it is coming and understand that it does not care about how much pain it causes. The silence is not assuaged by words; it is not persuaded by the presence of joy. It follows us, sits with us, and reminds us of that which we would rather forget.

Over time, silence begins to lose its potency but it never completely goes away. Silence is part of the grieving process and as there will always be loss, there will always be silence. If we can convince ourselves not to fight it but to recognize it and ride it, we may just survive. When caught in a dangerous riptide at the beach, swimmers are taught to relax and let it take you to a place where the current isn't so strong. To fight it is to let it take you farther out to sea as you become exhausted and drown.

Maybe we should learn to ride the current caused by grief. Only then will we slowly begin to hear the loving voices around us telling us that life goes on in spite of our loss and the hole it has caused.

Amen and amen.

DAY 71
ELBOW GREASE

I love you, O LORD, my strength. The LORD is my rock, my fortress, and my deliverer, my God, my rock in whom I take refuge, my shield, and the horn of my salvation, my stronghold. I call upon the LORD, who is worthy to be praised, so I shall be saved from my enemies.
—Psalm 18:1–3

One day when I was a little girl, one of my assigned chores was to scrub the kitchen floor. My mother did not believe in mops. "The only way to get a floor clean," she would say, "is to get on your hands and knees and scrub." While I didn't necessarily agree with her, I had no choice but to do as she directed me. So there I was, on my hands and knees, scrubbing.

On this particular day, I was scrubbing and there was a stain that would not come up. I decided it was stuck there and moved on.

My mother was watching me. As I moved away from the stain, she said, "Go back and get that stain up, Susan." I protested. "Mama! It won't come up!"

Mama said, "It will come up. For some dirt, you have to use *elbow grease.*"

For some dirt, you have to use elbow grease.

I took Mama's words literally and decided I needed to find the elbow grease. I got up and went to the bathroom, got on my stool, and looked in the medicine cabinet.

Mama came to the bathroom door. "What are you doing?" she asked.

I said, "Looking for the elbow grease."

Mama laughed, and said, "Silly, you already have it. The elbow grease is inside of you. It helps you do what you can't do all by yourself."

I have never forgotten that day, the stain itself, looking for the elbow grease, and going back to the kitchen floor, intrigued by what my mother had said. I scrubbed and scrubbed until, finally, that stubborn stain did come up.

God in us is our elbow grease. So many times in the Bible, we see the words, "The Lord is my strength."

The Lord within us is the elbow grease we need to get the stubborn stains off our souls, out of our memories, out of our view, and away from our hearing. Calling on the Lord when the stains are getting thicker and tougher is how we use the elbow grease within us. Some of the stains in our lives come up rather easily but there are more stubborn stains that stay with us, haunt us, and have the capacity to overwhelm us and take us down even further.

Calling on the Lord for the weaker stains is easy but calling on God when the stains are stubborn can drain our soul of hope and energy. That is when we must activate the "elbow grease." We call on the Lord with a depth and passion that is strong enough to get the stain up and out of our spirits.

It's called "elbow grease praying."

Amen and amen.

DAY 72

GIRD YOUR LOINS

A shatterer has come up against you. Guard the ramparts; watch the road; gird your loins; collect all your strength.
—Nahum 2:1

On a hot summer night in Detroit, my two sisters and I slept in one bedroom. The windows were open and there was a slight breeze that offered little comfort. Somehow, we slept soundly, despite the oppressive heat.

But on this particular night, our peaceful sleep was interrupted by loud cracking, like sticks breaking all around us. I was horrified. Our bedroom was filled with an orange glow—fire! Panicked, I woke my sisters and set off to wake my brothers. Our house was on fire and I wasn't sure what to do. What if we couldn't get out? What if Mama and Daddy, who slept downstairs, were trapped by flames? What if someone died? I rushed my siblings down the stairs and toward the front door.

As it turned out, our house was not on fire. But our neighbor's garage was. I was relieved; Mama and Daddy were at the foot of the stairs waiting for us, as our activity had awakened them. We all hurried out the front door.

That night, we were comfortably asleep, and then, suddenly, we were afraid. I have often thought of that night when I hear horrible news accounts of the brazenly racist words and actions of politicians. It's easy to reminisce about life under friendlier administrations, when *we were comfortable*. We are afraid of uncertainty. We are afraid that the flames near us are really *in* our houses.

In 2017, on the eve of the inauguration of Donald Trump, activist and scholar Angela Davis gave an interview in which she called Donald Trump's election "a last gasp of a dying white male supremacy." She spoke of a movement waking up. "I sense a feeling of solidarity," she said. "All the people I met on the way to the studio today were talking about how important it is going to be to engage in a continued fight over the next four years. So I'm very sad but I'm also excited because it appears as if we are witnessing... the fruits of the organizing week over the last years and decades even."[42]

In other words, we have been awakened from a place of comfort by flames that are close but from which we can escape. We have to wake those who are still asleep because we all need to go out the front door, away from the flames and the smoke, and toward justice.

In the book of Nahum, it says, *"A shatterer has come up against you. Guard the ramparts; watch the road; gird your loins; collect all*

42. "Inauguration 2017 Special Coverage w/ Angela Davis, Naomi Klein, Ralph Nader & More," Democracy Now, January 20, 2017, https://www.democracynow.org/live/inauguration_2017_live_coverage (accessed July 23, 2019).

your strength." The prophet was talking about the imminent destruction of the Assyrian Empire; Ninevah was going down. God had seen and God was coming. His warning: *"gird your loins; collect all your strength."*

Over the past several years, we have watched the unpeeling and undoing of fifty years of hard-fought civil rights progress. We have hunkered down in safe isolation as we learned to navigate the obstacle thrown up in front of us. Then Trayvvon Martin was killed and a movement began to brew. When Eric Garner was killed, the flames grew higher. Then came Michael Brown, Walter Scott, Freddie Gray, Laquan McDonald, Philando Castile, Antwon Rose, and others—each time, stoking the fires higher and higher. The cries against injustice on all levels grow louder and louder. Could it be that God, as in Nahum's day, is rising up against an oppressive empire? Could it be that the intensifying flames have a dual purpose of waking us and mobilizing us?

Whatever God is doing, it is clear that this is no time to retreat. Now is the time we "gird up our loins and collect all our strength," knowing that we are moving away from the flames that are close by but not close enough to overtake us. We are awakening; we have time to awaken others and get them to safety. The time for quiet sleep is over. The coming years will be a time to work, to resist, and to trust in the God who has always been in the midst of any and all struggles for justice.

We were comfortable. Maybe now, some of us are afraid. But all of us must gird up our loins.

Amen and amen.

DAY 73

SPIRITUAL DEHYDRATION

As the deer pants for streams of water,
so my soul pants for you, my God.
—Psalm 42:1 NIV

On July 5, 2016, Alton Sterling was selling CDs outside a convenience store in Baton Rouge, Louisiana. Moments later, police had wrestled him to the ground, straddled him, and shot him dead at point-blank range. There had been a report of a man in a red shirt using a gun to threaten someone. Sterling had started carrying a gun a few days prior to the event after being robbed by other CD vendors. In talking to reporters afterward, the owner of the convenience store said that Sterling was not the one causing trouble. The shooting was recorded by several bystanders.

Organizers and activists, pastors and priests, became responsible for trying to keep the black community from erupting in rage after yet another killing of a black man by police. The work of organizers is hard, but the work of pastors, priests, and other religious leaders can be far more difficult.

Religious leaders of the African American community are faced with aching questions reflecting frustration and pain: "Why?" "How long?" It's easy to know what not to say: "His ways are higher than our ways" or "God is good, all the time." Perhaps the best thing to say is to acknowledge that people are searching for God *"as the deer pants for streams of water"* (Psalm 42:1 NIV). They yearn for spiritual hydration for their justice-parched souls. For too long, they have been crawling across an arid desert of hopelessness when it comes to expecting racial justice in this country. They have cried so much they are nearly out of tears.

What will we do? How will we minister? We, like them, are panting as well. Our souls are just as dry as are theirs are. We squeeze our tears out and wrestle with anger.

And yet, hard as it seems, we must direct people back to God. We may not be able to proclaim how wonderful God is. We may be so wracked with our own questions that a sermon seems nearly impossible to preach, and yet, we must. That is the call. The call is to point others to the source of spiritual hydration.

Maybe it's best to talk this week about the *presence* of God. God is present in the time of great pain, in the time of great loss and great confusion, holding us up, giving us the very breath we take next. And in the conversation about God's presence, God will show up, as God does, giving us the strength to give to others ...yet one more time.

Amen and amen.

DAY 74
GOD IN THE TIME OF TROUBLE

Hear us, Shepherd of Israel, you who lead Joseph like a flock. You who sit enthroned between the cherubim, shine forth before Ephraim, Benjamin and Manesseh. Awaken your might; come and save us. Restore us, O God; make our face shine on us, that we may be saved.
—Psalm 80:1–3 NIV

In the quiet aftermath of tragedy, a question arises, "Where was God? Why couldn't—or didn't—our omnipotent God step in and stop this horrific thing from happening?"

What is prayer at a time like this? *"Hear us, Shepherd of Israel, you who lead Joseph like a flock."* We have been told that the Shepherd is always with us, that the Shepherd loves us. But the Shepherd also allows for pain, tragedy, and despair.

The people cry out to the Shepherd, who, too often, remains silent.

For the oppressed, the issue of God can be a difficult one; the God of the oppressed is the same as the God of the oppressor, and the God of the oppressed does not have a good track record at protecting the oppressed from the oppressor.

The God of the oppressed is all the oppressed have in the face of their suffering. Had it not been for their God, the oppressed would have given in to despair long ago. The God of the oppressed offers a Presence that overcomes evil by filling the oppressed with a strength the oppressor cannot begin to imagine. The oppressed are knocked down, kicked while they are down, but their God helps them get up, time after time. The God of the oppressed heals their bruises, stitches their cuts, and mends their broken bones.

If only the oppressor would come face-to-face with the God of the oppressed. In 1 Kings 18, the prophets of Baal came face-to-face with the God of the oppressed in the form of the prophet Elijah, who challenged them to call down fire from heaven. "Call your god!" Elijah said. When the prophets of Baal tried, nothing happened. But when Elijah called, the God of the oppressed showed up in the form of fire: *"Then the fire of the LORD fell and consumed the burnt offering, the wood, the stones, and the dust, and even licked up the water that was in the trench"* (1 Kings 18:38).

In life, despite the pain, tragedy, injustice, and cruelty, the God of the oppressed shows up.

What the God of the oppressed does *not* do is prevent injustice and evil from existing. So, yes, there is racism, sexism, homophobia, Islamophobia, militarism, capitalism, poverty, and materialism. God has allowed great evil to exist and, to be honest, sometimes we get angry about it.

But at the end of the day, it is God who allows the oppressed to walk on once-broken legs, to rise once more despite spirits that have been broken and mended. And it is the God of the oppressed who has restored us, giving us strength and light to fight the darkness of evil that is ever around us.

Amen and amen.

DAY 75
TREADING WATER

O taste and see that the LORD is good;
happy are those who take refuge in him.
—Psalm 34:8

When I was little, my mother would take my siblings and me to an amusement park. She frequently urged me to try the rides that were, in my view, "challenging." I gradually tried some of her recommendations but the one ride I would *not* try was the one in which you stood up and spun so fast that you were pinned to the wall as the floor fell down from under your feet.

My mother loved that ride and wanted me to experience its thrill, but I wasn't having it. I was concerned about falling into the pit. My mother would laugh and then explain that centrifugal force would keep me flattened on the wall until the speed of the ride got to a point where the floor came back up.

I still wasn't having it. I needed a floor under my feet. In fact, I never went on rides where my feet dangled. I needed to have something solid under my feet; otherwise, I felt too vulnerable.

I had the same feeling when swimming. I was a good swimmer but when I was urged to jump into deep water, I panicked. I had been taught to tread water but for some reason, not being able to feel the floor of the pool freaked me out.

I needed solid ground under my feet.

We want the security that solid ground provides. There is something unsettling about being unable to *feel* the ground that supports you. Many of us will not try new things because, metaphorically, we cannot feel the ground under our feet. We feel as though we are helpless in deep water, and that feeling is uncomfortable.

There are people who are willing to tread water, to step off the dock, leap from the canoe, jump from the airplane. These are folks who are able to *"taste and see that the LORD is good."* It is in our vulnerability, our places of weakness, that we experience the power and the majesty of God. When we can relax in the midst of deep water, we give God the ability to breathe God's own Spirit into us, providing us with the courage to continue treading and then to swim.

When we are emotionally distraught and our insides are churning, we are in deep water. We forget that instead of fighting it, we can relax and tread water.

Thinking about the depth of the issues in our lives holds us back. We let the things people say about us dissuade our courage. We give in to our fears and insecurities, which take over and make us believe that the water is deeper than it actually is. We allow the sounds and the challenges, our disappointments and failures, to stop us from venturing into water we falsely believe is too deep for us.

And yet, it is in the depths of our experiences that we most profoundly experience God. It is when we cannot stand on anything but God that we begin to *understand* what this life is about.

We who are safely waiting on solid ground are compelled to go into deep water, where we can gently encourage those who are floundering so that they can have an abundant life.

God wants us to *"taste and see that the LORD is good."* One of the best ways to do that is to jump into the deep waters of life and tread water until you can swim.

Amen and amen.

DAY 76
LOOKING FOR GOD FROM THE SIDEWALK

Those who wait for the LORD shall renew their strength, they shall mount up with wings like eagles, they shall run and not be weary, they shall walk and not faint.
—Isaiah 40:31

When I was a little girl, I lived with foster parents, Mama and Daddy McElrath. I never knew my birth father, and my mother was simply "away"—who knows where. But every two weeks, she would come to visit me at the McElraths' house. I was always excited to see her. Mama McElrath made me put on a dress, combed my hair, and put what seemed like a million ribbons in it. When it was nearly time for my mother's expected arrival, Mama McElrath would call out, "Susan, it's time for your mother to come home!" I would run outside and sit in the middle of the sidewalk, in my dress, facing the direction of the main street Mama walked to get to us. As soon as I saw her walking down the street, I would get up and run toward her, crying, "Mama! Mama!"

Even when I was sick and made to stay inside, I would not miss sitting on that sidewalk, in my dress, waiting for Mama. She was my life and I needed her.

Many of us are sitting in the middle of a sidewalk, all dressed up, and waiting for God. Or perhaps some of us have given up waiting. We became discouraged with life and all the waiting. Too many obstacles have been thrown in front of us; we have cried too many tears or lost our belief that God cares about us. Too many of us, even faithful church-goers, have given up on sitting in the middle of the sidewalk, waiting, expecting, and welcoming God into our lives.

Our human eyes can get in our way. We look for what we *wish* to see and fail to see what God *wants* us to see. Instead of waiting, we run toward the wrong person, the wrong opportunity, or the wrong voice.

There were times as I waited for my mother, sitting on that sidewalk, when I would get up to run because I thought she was coming down the street. But my eyes *knew* my mother and as I ran, my eyes recognized that it was not the woman who would welcome and love me. I walked back to the Mrs. McElrath's house, sat back down in the middle of the sidewalk, and waited.

In life, waiting gets tiresome. We tire of expecting and not receiving; we tire of being uncomfortable as we wait. There must be a reason that Isaiah wrote, *"Those who wait for the Lord shall renew their strength."* Isaiah knew that waiting is not a passive, but rather, an active endeavor with fits and starts, comings and goings, like the ebbing and flowing of the sea. We strain our eyes and try to make God into our image, conformed to our wants and needs, and we grow impatient as God remains God despite our protestations. Sometimes, we miss God altogether because, in our impatience, we have run not to the source of our help, but to a counterfeit source of disappointment.

When we look for God, when we are desperate for God to come to us, as I was desperate for my mother to come to me, eventually, we are honored with God's presence. God walks toward us and we, straining through eyes filled with tears, recognize God. Our spirits leap within us and tell us that it is time to run to God. As we run, God runs toward us, as happy to receive us as we are to find the comfort of God's presence. We leave the middle of the sidewalk and go to the Source of love and grace and mercy and forgiveness. We leave the front of the house and run toward the presence of the One who gives us complete comfort and care.

I don't remember my mother ever leaving the McElraths' house to go back to wherever she was going. Never once did she allow me to watch her walk out that door. The image I treasure is that of my mother walking, almost running, toward me as I run toward her, and of her holding my hand as we walk into the house together.

God is walking toward us, hand outstretched. God, give us eyes to see so we can leave the middle of the sidewalk and run to the Source of our strength.

Amen and amen.

DAY 77
IT IS SCARY TO LOVE

Beloved, let us love one another, because love is from God; everyone who loves is born of God and knows God.
—1 John 4:7

When we are young, we live in a world that life has not yet touched. We believe what is will always be. We understand that there are old people and young people but we do not understand that those whom we love, whose faces are deeply wrinkled and who struggle to walk, were once young and vibrant. We do not think that we could lose anyone we love; in our immature minds, those who are around us will always be there.

But as we get older, life does indeed touch us. We experience disappointment, unfairness, fear of failure, and even fear of success. We begin to see that life is not static but is, rather, a dynamic force in which things happen that are not always pleasing or fair.

We learn that to love is glorious but also risky. We learn that love can hurt. And we learn that those whom we love can be taken from us.

The poet Yehuda Halevi summed this up in his poem, "'Tis a Fearful Thing." He beautifully captured what love feels like when we understand the risk involved.

'Tis a fearful thing
To love what death can touch.
A fearful thing
To love, to hope, to dream, to be—
To be, and oh, to lose.

A thing for fools, this,
And a holy thing,
A holy thing to love.
For your life has lived in me,
Your laugh once lifted me,
Your word was gift to me.
To remember this brings painful joy.
'Tis a human thing, love,
A holy thing, to love,
What death has touched.

Only the young can love without fear. When we are young, we yearn to possess those we love and exact a promise that they will always be there. But that is not how life works. Life snatches our loved ones away without warning or thought.

As we get older, we realize with sadness that those whom we have loved—parents, siblings, spouses, friends—people with whom we have spent precious moments and have precious memories, will all leave us…unless we leave them first.

Loss is a major part of love.

It is scary to love because love demands our hearts. An older woman once told me that she thought she was in love with a gentleman who was older than her but she was afraid to love him because "he is old enough that I think he could die soon." Because of that fear, she chose not to invest herself. "I can't take the thought of him not being around," she said.

Where would we be if God was afraid to love us simply because we might disappoint, betray, or leave Her? To be loved and to love is, as Halevi said, "a holy thing." To know and to feel the power of love, even if the object of that love is snatched away far too soon, is to know God. What or who we love is never permanent; death hovers over us all but if we don't take a risk, we rob ourselves of that which begins with and emanates from God, and that is love.

Amen and amen.

DAY 78
OUR HONEST AND TROUBLING STRUGGLE WITH GOD

I will not restrain my mouth; I will speak in the anguish of my spirit; I will complain in the bitterness of my soul. …Why have you made me your target? Why have I become a burden to you?
—Job 7:11, 20

We do not often talk about our honest and sometimes troubling struggle with God. For many, just to admit such a struggle reveals a weakened faith, and nobody wants to admit that. But the truth is, a relationship with God includes struggle—a struggle to understand unfathomable mysteries we may never comprehend and to grow our faith in spite of hardship and pain.

Struggling with God often leads to the expression of righteous anger. Job, feeling wronged by God, cried out *"in the anguish of my spirit"* and *"in the bitterness of my soul."* Job demanded, *"Why have you made me a target?"* In our anguish, we cry out, "Why did You do this? Why would You let this happen? Why do you allow this kind of persecution?"

A long time ago, when I was a nursing student, I was assigned to give care to a fourteen-year-old girl who had been severely burned in a house fire. I was academically equipped to deal with her pain; I knew that changing the dressings on her burns would be excruciating. I knew I would have to make sure her fluid intake was adequate. But I was not prepared for her emotional and spiritual pain due to her disappointment and anger at God.

We built a relationship. I fought back tears as I endured the screams when her burns were debrided and her dressings were changed. One of her ears was gone, as was one of her eyes. She had little to no hair left. Her body looked like a mangled piece of paper. She was not allowed to look into a mirror. Not fully aware of the extent of her wounds, she would express her desire to one day be an airline stewardess—the old name for flight attendants.

Her mother cornered me one day. "She is wrestling with God," her mother said. "She has been asking why God let this happen to her. What should I say? I don't understand it myself." I certainly didn't have an answer.

She had been a vibrant child with deep faith in God. She believed God was going to take away her pain and scars. One day, she asked if I believed God would do that. I was silent for a minute. I didn't know if her pain would ever go away. I was fairly sure her scarring wouldn't.

She waited for my answer. I didn't have one that would please her. Finally, I said, "All I know is that God is with you. Whatever you go through from this day forward, God will be with you."

She was not impressed, and shot back, "Why wasn't God with me in the fire? Why did God let this happen to me?"

Her questions reflected the bitterness of her soul, like so many others who have endured, or continue to endure, unimaginable pain due to random accidents or the capacity of human beings to render evil to each other.

In my upbringing, questioning God was not permitted. But we all question God at times. We relate not only to the suffering of Job but also to the words of the psalmist, who wrote, "*Do not fret because of the wicked; do not be envious of wrongdoers*" (Psalm 37:1). In order to survive and thrive in this world, we must not put ourselves down for wondering, from time to time, where God is. God is able to withstand our wailing. We *must* acknowledge our struggles so we can remain connected to the only Source of strength to endure evil.

We will never understand how God works or why God allows suffering, but we will always have the blessed assurance that God will keep us sane as we pick up our crosses and follow Her. We will always have moments when we deal with the bitterness in our souls. In those times, it is the ability to honestly struggle with God that will allow us to confront evil, discomfort, and pain, and thus, confound those people or situations that desire to rob us of our joy.

Amen and amen.

DAY 79
REACHING FOR THE TRANSCENDENT

O the depth of the riches and wisdom and knowledge of God! How unsearchable are his judgments and how inscrutable his ways! "For who has known the mind of the Lord? Or who has been his counselor? Or who has given a gift to him, to receive a gift in return?" For from him and through him and to him are all things. To him be the glory forever.
—Romans 11:33–36

The late Mircea Eliade, professor of the history of religion at the University of Chicago, once wrote, "Life is not possible without an opening toward the transcendent."

But how do we reach for the transcendent in a time of personal and social suffering?

The definition of *transcendent*, according to *The Oxford Dictionary*, is "beyond or above the range of normal or merely human experience...surpassing the ordinary." As pertains to God, I would define *transcendent* as existing apart from and not subject to the limitations of the material universe. Today, it seems that some people are reaching for the transcendent in order to rise above the political chaos that exists in this country.

The faith of many is being tested these days. The political divisiveness and vengeful attacks on immigration, LGBTQ rights, women's rights, health care, and environmental protections, as well as the dismantling of Civil Rights legislation, has created social suffering that has, in turn, increased the personal suffering of many. Many cannot reconcile what is going on with the notion of a "good" God.

Black people in America have learned to reach for and believe in the transcendent. This capacity has enabled them not only to hold on but to thrive, to keep on moving, despite all efforts to slow us down or eliminate us.

The events of the past decade reveal the fact that white supremacy is pervasive; this system seeks to destroy not only black people but any and all who are not a part of the elite club of wealthy, white, heterosexual, Protestant men. Nobody is safe—not women, not people of color, not the LGBTQ community, not the poor, and not the elderly.

What would God have us do? This is not a time to sit in despair; it is a time to look ever more intentionally for the transcendent. It is not a time to retreat into safe shells of personal piety but a time to come out of our safe places and stand up against the powers and principalities that are brazenly working to undo the faith of the people of God.

Poet Langston Hughes said it best: "Life for us ain't been no crystal stair." Nevertheless, reaching for and believing in the transcendent has saved our lives. And it is reaching toward the transcendent that will ultimately save all those whose eyes are opening for the first time to reach for the God of weary years and silent tears.

The transcendent awaits our attempt to reach for it, and God, in the midst of all of this madness, reaches back. Today, reach and stretch past the evil around us. God is there.

Amen and amen.

DAY 80
SPIRITUAL MALPRACTICE

I will raise up shepherds over them who will shepherd them, and they shall not fear any longer, or be dismayed, nor shall any be missing, says the LORD.
—Jeremiah 23:4

At a recent gathering of preachers, pastors, theologians, and academicians, Rev. Dr. William Bobby McClain, Professor of Preaching and Worship at Wesley Theological Seminary said, "There has to be a prophetic witness and a spiritual holiness. If both are not present, the preacher ought to be charged with spiritual malpractice."

Spiritual malpractice.

In a time of spiritual trauma caused by social injustice, Dr. McClain's words are biting and appropriate.

Many preachers prefer not to touch the "hot potato" issues that are boiling in the stew of American culture. The pot is brimming with the ingredients of our society: racism, immigration, sexism, homophobia, xenophobia, poverty, mass incarceration, health care...and that's only the beginning. This is a recipe that makes America what it is.

To ignore the smell of an overcooked stew that has been left on the fire for too long is to ignore the cries of people who hunger for justice. It is not enough to say, "God is good." When a child is murdered, when a parent cannot make ends meet despite working two or three jobs, when a family files for bankruptcy because they can't afford to pay their medical bills, despair reigns. It fills our pews, and if we who preach ignore it, souls will begin to die for lack of spiritual nourishment.

What does the preacher do when he or she is likewise spiritually depleted? The dried-out soul has the responsibility of bringing living water to those who are also dried out. Gardner Taylor once told Dr. McClain that, in terms of what preachers do, "it is the guilty one telling guilty ones about the just cause of God."

The dried-out guilty ones must find a bit of spiritual sustenance, no matter how minuscule, in order to ease the trauma and despair of those sitting in the pews. If we ignore the difficult issues because we don't want to deal with them, because we are afraid of ruffling feathers, or because, frankly, we cannot find God ourselves, we are committing spiritual malpractice.

Those who preach and teach God in the midst of trying times must bring enough droplets of living water to share with those who need God. Those who preach and teach must make sure the vital signs of those seeking hope and peace and answers from God do not fail. Those who preach and teach must do everything possible to make sure that living water is circulating throughout the souls of the faithful, despite the dryness all around them.

In so doing, preachers bring God to the pews...a transfusion of hope from pulpit to pew, which is God being merciful, as only God can be. In that moment, there is prophetic witness and a spiritual holiness—evil and social injustice notwithstanding. Society and its evils create the wounds; preachers diagnose the spiritual condition and perform the surgery; God miraculously heals the scars.

Amen and amen.

DAY 81
WHEN YOU'RE EXPECTED TO GRIN AND BEAR IT

There is no longer Jew or Greek, there is no longer slave or free, there is no longer male and female; for all of you are one in Christ Jesus.
—Galatians 3:28

It has always puzzled me why some white people have railed against the so-called "angry black person"—male or female. How in the world can any person expect people who have been marginalized, humiliated, dehumanized, and criminalized to be happy about their situation?

It is the arrogance of power that gives this irrational thinking its place. When enslaved Africans—and later, native-born African Americans—sought their freedom, many slave owners were surprised, even hurt. They would say, "We treat our nigras good," perhaps meaning they beat them less than other owners and that they were "clothed and fed."

In 2016, first lady Michelle Obama remarked that she lived in a house built by slaves—the White House. Fox News host Bill O'Reilly dismissed her statement, insisting that America's slaves had been well fed and given adequate lodging. O'Reilly just couldn't imagine why they would feel discontent.[43]

Expecting the oppressed to "grin and bear" their treatment is not a new reality but it still makes no sense. It comes from the need of the oppressor to deflect guilt by dehumanizing those whom he or she oppresses. It is a desperate attempt to avoid any feelings of empathy or responsibility.

In my days as a nursing student, we were taught how to do intramuscular injections. My instructor taught us to "push the needle in harder" for African American patients because their skin was tougher. I practiced and practiced on an orange with thick skin so that when I had an African American patient, I would be able to do the injection correctly. When that day finally came, I was prepared to give the injection the way I had been taught, but lo and behold, as I jammed the needle into her arm, I realized her black skin was no different from the skin of my white patients.

Oppression is not only racial. It is also doled out in the form of sexism, ageism, homophobia, xenophobia, and classism. The

43. Daniel Victor, "Bill O'Reilly Defends Comments About 'Well Fed' Slaves," *New York Times*, July 27, 2016 https://www.nytimes.com/2016/07/28/business/media/bill-oreilly-says-slaves-who-helped-build-white-house-were-well-fed.html (accessed July 24, 2019).

poor—no matter their race or sex—are treated abominably in this country and throughout the world, yet they are expected to be thankful for what they are being given.

Jesus the Christ identified with the oppressed and spoke out against oppression in all its forms. He made His oppressors uncomfortable because He was not willing to "grin and bear it." Nor should any oppressed person be willing. The divine in all of us pushes against the command to be satisfied with being treated poorly; that same divine pushes in love and respect, but pushes nonetheless. Not to push against oppression means we relegate ourselves to living lives of what Henry David Thoreau called "quiet desperation," which, truly, cannot be the will of the God who made us all and said, "It is good."

Amen and amen.

DAY 82
THE DEPTH OF THE EXCELLENCE OF GOD

O LORD, our Sovereign, how majestic is your name in all the earth!
You have set your glory above the heavens. Out of the mouths of
babes and infants you have founded a bulwark because of your foes,
to silence the enemy and the avenger. When I look at your heavens,
the work of your fingers, the moon and the stars that you have
established; what are human beings that you are mindful of them,
mortals that you care for them?
—Psalm 8:1–4

The declaration of God's excellence is captured in Psalm 8: "O LORD, our Sovereign, how majestic is your name in all the earth." After Psalm 23, my mother required us to learn Psalm 8. "There's nobody and nothing greater or grander than God," she would say.

She would make us look at the sky at night—I mean, *make us* look up, *make us* notice the constellations, and say, "You can't go through life not knowing how great God is." One night, I decided I would try to count the stars, and she just laughed…but she let me try. I think I had gotten to about a hundred, thinking that was a lot of stars, surely, and Mama said, "That's why God is so great. God has stars in places no human will ever see."

The facts of science bear her out. There are more stars, it says in *Scientific American*, than words ever uttered by all the humans who ever lived.[44]

Who cares? Who cares about the magnificence of God, the depth of God's excellence? We should, because surely, a God who created more stars than words ever uttered by all the humans who ever lived is a God who can handle our pain, our questions, our struggles, our issues. If we stopped and concentrated on the magnificence of God, and on what God has done, we would relinquish doubt and anxiety that restricts us. We would develop a trust in God that would transfer over into our work to build God's kingdom on this earth…and that would be pleasing to God.

This God cannot be put into a box, but we try to do that. We try to stuff God into our realities, instead of allowing God to usher us into God's reality. The psalmist knew it. He wrote, *"When I look at your heavens, the work of your fingers, the moon and the stars that you have established; what are human beings that you are mindful of them, mortals that you care for them?"* It is singularly amazing, and an honor that God thinks of us as worthy of divine time. God is willing to give God's self to us, but we so often reject the divine

44. Lawrence Rifkin, "10 Sublime Wonders of Science," ScientificAmerican.com, October 8, 2013, https://blogs.scientificamerican.com/guest-blog/10-sublime-wonders-of-science/ (accessed July 25, 2019).

overtures that would help us cope with what is going on in our personal lives and in the world.

As God has stars in places that no human will ever see, so God has answers that we cannot imagine and will not access unless we stop and consider the depth of God's excellence. We as human beings have given the "-isms" of life way too much power, even as we have marginalized God, but if we relinquish our control, God will do what God is divinely equipped to do. There is no racism, no sexism, no homophobic attitude that God cannot handle. There is no personal pain that God cannot help us through. If we stop long enough to look at the heavens, and declare the excellence of God—once a day—perhaps we can draw closer to God and give God room to draw closer to us so that we can benefit from God's presence in ways we have not yet realized.

In the presence of God, we are allowed to see the expanse of God's excellence. It is more mighty and impressive than anything money can buy or the human mind can imagine. The issues of life—God can handle. God knows that…but God wants us to know that as well.

Inhale the beauty of God's holiness and the depth of God's excellence. Exhale the doubt and the need to be in control…and rest in the only arms that can keep us intact in the midst of a very broken world.

Amen and amen.

DAY 83

THE FATAL FLAW OF SEEKING VENGEANCE

For we know the one who said, "Vengeance is mine, I will repay."
And again, "The Lord will judge his people."
—Hebrew 10:30

There is a story about God watching the Israelites as they were being pursued by the Egyptians. The angels watched anxiously as the drama unfolded, wondering what God would do. When God parted the waters of the Sea of Reeds, the angels broke out in applause. God had saved the "good guys" and killed the "bad" ones. The angels celebrated.

But their celebration was cut short as they observed that God was *not* celebrating. The angels were confused, and asked God, "Aren't you happy? You saved Your people," but the morose God answered quietly, "Yes, but did you see how many of my people I had to kill?"

This is a story my mother used to tell us when we were children. "Bad things will happen to you," she said, "and you will do bad things, too, which will hurt people, but you never seek revenge. You let God do that. God is not happy when any of His children suffer, and God isn't happy when we try to do what only God can do."

The difference in what God does and what we do when seeking revenge is that God chastises with a sense of parental love. Earthly parents sigh and become sad, or angry, or both, as they try to get wayward children to do right and there are times when they have to discipline them. How many of us remember hearing, right before we were spanked, "This is going to hurt me more than it hurts you?" The statement sounded ludicrous to me and my siblings, but as we grew older, we learned that discipline is a part of love. Our parents hurt when they had to discipline us, and so does God, but no matter how disappointed or sad or angry a parent—divine or spiritual—becomes, in the end, they love their children, no matter what, and want the best for them. Except in cases of child abuse, the discipline is done for our good, and our parents and our God both regret that they have to bring us some discomfort at times.

Our impulse is to strike someone who has struck us—harder, if possible—so we can see them suffer as they have made us suffer. We believe seeing them suffer will make us feel better, but it does not, because it only creates fodder for a more permanent battlefield, with each offensive becoming more and more brutal. God seeks to change the hearts of those who offend, not injure them further. God feels compassion for *us* when we do wrong, and God *feels the same compassion for those who have done us wrong*.

When Cain murdered Abel, God was disturbed. Cain immediately becomes afraid that others will want to hurt him, seeking revenge because of what he has done to his brother, but God says, "No. Not so! Whoever kills Cain will suffer a sevenfold vengeance!" And then God put a mark on Cain so nobody would be able to kill him. (See Genesis 4.)

God puts a "mark" on us, to protect us when we have done wrong, and God likewise puts a mark on those who have done us wrong. God chastises with love and with the hope that there will be a change. God's justice is restorative, not punitive. God's justice seeks for us to grow, not for us to slide into caverns of guilt, shame, and fear.

It is maddening to think that God can and does love us all. God loves political leaders who wreak havoc over the entire world; God loves racist lawmakers and religious leaders who do more to defame the name of God than to uplift it. God loved my mama and God loved Alabama Gov. George Wallace. God loves me and the ones whom I have offended. The job of seeking justice (which is what we call our efforts at revenge) belongs to God, and God alone.

Those who do not understand this part of God make their lives miserable by seeking revenge, but they also contribute to the never-ending cycle of violence. We say "an eye for an eye," quoting Hammurabi's code, but Dr. Martin Luther King reminded us that with such a formula, eventually everyone will be blind.

We have no control over what our religious and political leaders do, but we have the opportunity to practice giving our issues to God and letting God seek the revenge (justice) we desire. God will do it. Our job is to believe that and rest in that belief.

As is frequently preached, "Won't He do it?"

The answer: "Yes, God will."

Amen and amen.

DAY 84
THE GIFT AND FUNCTION OF "UNSTRUCTURED MALEVOLENCES"

We…boast in our sufferings, knowing that suffering produces endurance, and endurance produces character, and character produces hope, and hope does not disappoint us, because God's love has been poured into our hearts through the Holy Spirit that has been given to us.
—Romans 5:3–5

In *The Inward Journey*, Howard Thurman wrote, "The stirring of energy in myriad forms of unstructured malevolences may well be the spirit of Life, of God at work in behalf of new life and perhaps a new creation on this planet."[45]

This sentence stopped me cold, because clearly, there are "unstructured malevolences" going on all around us. We are being bombarded by storms, both physical and political, that are ripping us from our berths of comfort and familiarity and thrusting us into a space of mystery and the unknown. As I write this, our nation is suffering from the malevolence of the people at the top of the federal government and its agencies; people are weary of tweets and name-calling and the overt racial bias in our national rhetoric. At times, our government has seemed to be a spectacle, an ongoing reality show. America has become the laughing stock of the world but worse, a symbol of ignorance and bigotry.

Political storms are thrusting us backward, it seems, to a time and place we wanted to believe were long gone. Our very lives are being tossed and blown; we are being beaten down by winds of oppression, racism, sexism, ignorance, arrogance, homophobia, nationalism, racial identity politics, and more. The gains of "the least of these" are being reversed with no regard for those who will be most seriously affected.

Unstructured malevolences are all around us.

Thurman said we must "find our place in the areas of new vitalities, the place where the old is breaking up and the new is being born."[46] Perhaps we are in a process of growing—the unstructured malevolences are planting new seeds within us and within our society. These seeds will bring forth new life. Surely, no one can hold on

---

45. Thurman, *The Inward Journey*, 107.
46. Ibid, 107–108.

to "what was" and maintain sanity. The loss of what we knew is too great to bear. No, the way to get through periods of unstructured malevolences is to accept that something new is being born. Instead of looking back to what was, times like these force us to look forward to see "what the end will bring."

It is not possible to "understand God." Those of us who try to intellectualize what is beyond our capacity to grasp run the danger of slipping into despair. If we say God is sovereign, we must accept God's sovereignty in all of its components.

Unstructured malevolences are a part of God's sovereignty. We may not like it. They may feel scary and may make us angry or doubt God. Our comfortable faith takes a hit when these malevolences come...but perhaps a shaken and done-over faith is what God wants us to have. Perhaps a comfortable and complacent faith denotes death and therefore, seeds of newness have to be planted in order to bring forth a strengthened faith, a faith that can and will weather the malevolences in a way that will honor God.

We are taught that "God is good, all the time." When unstructured malevolences hit us, we may forget that—but it is at that very time we must *not* forget. In the space where we have nothing but our memory and notion of a "good God," those memories must well up and fill the space...and in doing so, give us the spiritual oxygen and nutrients we will need to make it through to the other side.

The gift and the function of "unstructured malevolences" is new life. In spite of the pain and misery, the malevolences indicate a period of labor that will lead to the birth of the newness God wants. Somehow, we must remember that.

Amen and amen.

DAY 85

UNDERSTANDING SOUL POVERTY

*Ho, everyone who thirsts, come to the waters; and you that have no
money, come, buy and eat! Come, buy wine and milk without money
and without price. Why do you spend your money for that which
is not bread, and your labor for that which does not satisfy? Listen
carefully to me, and eat what is good, and delight yourselves in rich
food. Incline your ear, and come to me; listen, so that you may live.*
—Isaiah 55:1–3

I read in Lisa Sharon Harper's book, *The Very Good Gospel*, that
people in Haiti are so poor they eat mud. Specifically, she writes,
"To get by, the poorest of the poor have taken to eating mud. Pat-
ties made of mud, oil, and sugar calm the stomachs of hungry humans."[47]

It occurred to me that the physical poverty we can see with our
eyes replicates the soul poverty we cannot see. There are those of us
"eating mud," meaning our souls are starved of the capacity to *"taste
and see that the LORD is good"* (Psalm 34:8). Too many of us do not
see it, or believe it. A clergy friend of mine, whose stepmother is
dying a horrific death due to cancer, asked me, "Does God care? Is
God present?" When we get to those places in our spiritual walk, we
are, in effect, "eating mud," consuming the elements of life that allow
us to survive but not to thrive, and certainly not to realize the power
and potential God put within us all.

What causes soul poverty? It is different than mental illness,
which responds to treatment and medication. Soul poverty comes

---

47. Lisa Sharon Harper, *The Very Good Gospel: How Everything Wrong Can Be Made
Right* (New York: WaterBrook, 2016), 104.

from the vicissitudes of life for which there are no pills, and which no medical doctor can fix. Soul poverty comes from being beaten down by powers and principalities that desire to shred our spirits and make us doubt the power and presence of God. When our souls are poor, we cannot see the beauty of God's holiness. Poor souls ingest and digest the lies that people have told us about ourselves. Hearing those things is not the problem. The problem is that we have *accepted* and *digested* what they said. The seeds of our souls' poverty were planted when we were very young, and few of us recognized the problem.

In spite of going to church, even to a good church, where the preaching and the teaching and the music are all good, too many of us are still eating mud. We are getting by, living on the underside of life. We drink too much, eat too much, and gamble too much. We make feeble attempts to lift soul poverty, but nothing works… nothing, that is, but being close enough to God to be honest with ourselves.

When our souls are so poor that we "eat mud," we put blinders on our spiritual eyes and plugs in our ears so we cannot see or hear *ourselves*. To get off the garbage heaps, we must look inside of ourselves to see where the seeds of soul poverty were planted. We have to see them, and dig them up. We have to come face to face with those seeds, and, as we dig them up, become determined to keep digging them up until they are out. We have to look at the disease those seeds have caused, and risk feeling the pain that comes with rooting them out. We have to bear the stench of the part of our soul that has rotted, because those little seeds, which we chose to ignore, are like cancer, starting small and spreading throughout our bodies. It is not pleasant to go to the source of our soul's poverty. It does not feel good, but if we can do that, if we can risk moving away from the garbage heaps, we can begin a liberating and exhilarating journey. We will be able to see God in a new way; we will be able to *taste and see that the LORD is good,*" in spite of the work of the demons within us to convince us otherwise.

Lord, in Your mercy, help us move from the garbage heaps.

Amen and amen.

DAY 86
WHAT ELEPHANTS TEACH US

> *Therefore, since we are surrounded by so great a cloud of witnesses, let us also lay aside every weight and the sin that clings so closely, and let us run with perseverance the race that is set before us.*
> —Hebrews 12:1

The beatitude says, *"Blessed are those who mourn, for they will be comforted"* (Matthew 5:4). According to notes in the *New Revised Standard Bible,* the word *"blessed"* means to be "happy" or "satisfied," and that happiness and/or satisfaction comes to those who believe because in all things, in all situations, God is there, comforting, supporting, and helping.

One of the sources of great pain for human beings is mourning the loss of a loved one. The mourning process is cruel; it gives those who mourn brief times of relief but also invades their hard-fought-for peace at a moment's notice. You might believe you have gotten through the worst of it, only to be lambasted by some unforeseen trigger, which thrusts you back into the rough arms of grief. Grief holds on to us for far too long—or maybe we hold on to grief. Either way, the pain is immense and the duration of the grieving process is far too long for far too many.

While many believe that it is best to try to "move on," perhaps we should examine how we move on, how we treat those who have passed over. Maybe our grief would not be so painful if we felt like it was okay to *truly* grieve…and in that process, "take care" of the one whom we have lost.

Elephants do just that. Elephants are highly intelligent and communal, and they take care of each other, *even after death*. Mother elephants—and the elephant clan—show grief when a baby elephant is stillborn. When elephants come across the skeletal remains of another elephant, they stop. They are known to caress the bones of the dead elephant, and they hover over those bones, sometimes for days. They take some bones and tusks away and bury them, covering them with twigs, leaves, and dirt. They protect their own from predators, even after death. They walk away only after they feel like they have taken sufficient care of the body. Their mourning is assuaged by their capacity to care for their "friend," even after death.

In our society, we are taught to "move on" after a death, but the cloud of witnesses is ever over us, affecting our lives, our thoughts, moves, and actions, even if we do not recognize or acknowledge it. When my daughter Caroline graduated from Spelman College and all of us went out for dinner, I felt compelled, before saying the grace, to acknowledge her grandmother, her father's mother, by name. Jeanne Allen had been a presence in Caroline's life. She had been proud of her, and every time something significant happened in her life, Jeanne Allen had been there.

She may have been gone, but at that dinner, it felt like she was there, or like we had come upon her "remains." I lifted her name up and it took away some of my own sadness. We were taking care of her, even in death. We were covering her remains and taking them to a safe place. The silence at the table was stark at first, but then, as her presence was acknowledged, there was a collective breath of…something…maybe peace? Comfort? Both? Whatever it was, it was noticeable. It was present.

Maybe we should be like the elephants, and "take care" of the remains of our loved ones who are now in the cloud of witnesses. Maybe we should light a candle at our tables, and bring the loved ones to the meal, telling our children the story of who they were and what they meant to us, in essence, to *bind them as a sign on your hand, fix them as an emblem on your forehead* (Deuteronomy 6:8).

The elephants teach us that the presence of a loved one is not gone just because of death; they teach us that, even in the bones, their spirit is still active, still alive, still a part of this earth, still giving, and still reaching. Still.

Amen and amen.

DAY 87
YET DO WE MARVEL

Oh LORD…. When I look at your heavens, the work of your fingers, the moon and the stars that you have established; what are human beings that you are mindful of them, mortals that you care for them? Yet you have made them a little lower than God, and crowned them with glory and honor. You have given them dominion over the works of your hands; you have put all things under their feet, all sheep and oxen, and also the beasts of the field, the birds of the air, and the fish of the sea, whatever passes along the paths of the seas. O LORD, our Sovereign, how majestic is your name in all the earth!
—Psalm 8:1, 3–9

The poet Countee Cullen wrestled, as do all of us, with the question of where God might be found in the midst of abject injustice. His poem, "Yet Do I Marvel," captured his questions and his struggle:

> I doubt not God is good, well meaning, kind,
> And did He stoop to quibble, could tell why
> The buried mole continues blind,
> Why flesh that mirror Him must some day die.
> Make plain the reason tortured Tantalus
> Is baited by the fickle fruit, declare
> If merely brute caprice dooms Sisyphus
> To struggle up a never-ending stair.
> Inscrutable His ways are, and immune
> To catechism by a mind too strewn
> With petty cares to slightly understand
> What awful brain compels His awful hand.
> Yet do I marvel at this curious thing,
> To make a poet black, and bid him sing.

It surely puzzles the mind, which wrestles with the notion of an omniscient, omnipresent, omnipotent God and why evil and injustice can persist and flourish in spite of this kind of God. Because of the uniqueness of this God, every single snowflake that falls from the sky is different; there are no duplicates. Every single stripe on every single tiger is different. Every single human being, billions of us, are distinguishable by the structure of our faces, the placement and color of our eyes. Every single person's voice is different, in spite of there being just one larynx within us all. This God made a universe that we cannot begin to understand, with a depth and expanse we have not begun to penetrate. Marvel? How can we not?

Who can doubt that this God is *"excellent,"* as Psalm 8 states so eloquently?

And yet, evil sits in our midst. Evil and injustice rub against our wearied and scarred spirits, making us bleed and feel the pain of new scrapes on top of old ones. We have scabs from having fought injustice, torn open by the constant and persistent revisitation of evil upon us. There is no running from it. *"Where can I flee from your presence?"* asks the psalmist in Psalm 139:7, but we can ask the same question of evil. "Where can we flee from you? Wherever we go, you are there. Yes, God is there...but so are you." Injustice and evil are unwelcome intruders into our lives, and our magnificent God allows these intruders to stay amongst us.

In October 2016, the mother of Kalief Browder died. Her young son had spent three years in Rikers Island after being falsely accused of stealing someone's backpack. Kalief was held at Rikers awaiting a trial because his family could not afford three thousand dollars to bail him out. He refused a plea deal because, he said, he had not done anything wrong. In prison, he was beaten by inmates and guards alike. At the time of his arrest, he was sixteen years old. He spent nearly two of his three years of incarceration in solitary confinement. A year after his release, Kalief committed suicide. An article describing his mother's death said she died of a broken heart. Her heart was broken, both from his wrongful imprisonment and, of course, from his suicide.

People go through this kind of injustice every day, and yet, these bruised, battered, and belittled people continue to push forward, singing, because to not sing would mean they would cease to breathe and thus to live.

Who knows why God allows the injustice and cruelty? We must all marvel at the fact that in spite of everything, people continue to be born, to fight against evil, and to push through. People continue to create new beauty of their own human spirits, in spite of being taunted and pulled by evil.

Poets are still being born and prophets are still singing. Yes, we do marvel. We do, indeed.

Amen and amen.

DAY 88

KEEPING VIGIL AT THE BEDSIDE OF THE WORLD

I say to God, my rock, "Why have you forgotten me? Why must I walk about mournfully because the enemy oppresses me?" As with a deadly wound in my body, my adversaries taunt me, while they say to me continually, "Where is your God?" Why are you cast down, O my soul, and why are you disquieted within me? Hope in God; for I shall again praise him, my help and my God.
—Psalm 42:9–11

Howard Thurman noted that humans "keep a troubled vigil at the bedside of the world."[48] Those words are particularly striking when combined with the words of James Baldwin, in a 1970 interview with David Frost: "It is horrible to watch a nation lose itself." In that same interview, Baldwin bemoaned what he saw as the failure of the civil rights movement of the 1960s. He said, "In the beginning, we thought there was a way to reach the conscience of the people of this country." That optimism faded with time, Baldwin noted.

It was as though Baldwin was explaining why African Americans and other minorities were still keeping vigil—troubled

---

48. Thurman, *The Inward Journey*, 128.

vigil—at the bedside of the world. The powers that be have insisted on refusing the soul-therapy necessary to move beyond the evil of oppression, which, like a deadly virus, is overtaking all of our vital organs and causing them to shut down.

The world is indeed sick because we refuse to give God the honor and respect God deserves. We take God's presence for granted, even as we disrespect and ignore the things God cares about. We mutilate that which God has created and think nothing of it. In operating this way, it is as though we are taking an aspirin to treat a brain tumor. It just will not work. Some continue this behavior without a thought, while others see what is going on and know that the world is undergoing a seismic shift.

We are keeping a troubled vigil.

The only cure is God's true presence, and a genuine love and respect for the God who does not sanction what we are doing to each other and to the world God created. Our quest for material wealth has put us in a stock-market-like environment, screaming at each other, pushing each other aside, even breaking into fights, not because we love God's world but because we want to continue to exploit God's world by exploiting each other.

Some ask, as did the writer of Psalm 42, "Why is all of this happening? Why is evil in the form of racism and sexism and homophobia and transphobia and all of the other phobias happening? Where is your God? Why is God letting this happen?"

Those keeping vigil at the bedside of the world can only whisper, "We thought there was a way to reach the conscience of the people." The spiritual decay that began long ago only grows more and more putrid. Even if we tried to explain why we know God is present in spite of the world's sickness, far too many people would not understand. They would not be able to see or to hear.

Baldwin noted that this nation was "losing itself." We sit at our nation's bedside today as it appears to be losing itself and keep a troubled vigil, as God does the same. God calls us to listen and to work even as we hold vigil. We weep as we remember the goodness of the Lord in our lives but we also rejoice because, ultimately, we know the goodness of the Lord is stronger than the evil of the world. God has not forsaken us; God will be with us when this horrendous virus breaks; God will prevail.

Amen and amen.

DAY 89
BELIEVING WE CAN DO ALL THINGS

[Jesus] *said to them, "Because of your little faith. For truly I tell you, if you have faith the size of a mustard seed, you will say to this mountain, 'Move from here to there,' and it will move; and nothing will be impossible for you."*
—Matthew 17:20

Sometimes, we struggle with believing in humans' capacity to transcend obstacles. Every day, people born with physical, mental, economic, and social hardships shatter the world's low expectations of them by excelling in areas of athletics, academics, the arts, and business.

Beethoven began noticing buzzing in his ears at age twenty-six yet he composed many of his greatest works after going completely deaf at the age of forty-four. Stevie Wonder's blindness did not stop him from winning twenty-five Grammy Awards for his music. In 1921, Bessie Coleman, born to sharecroppers and a student at segregated schools, became the first woman of African American descent to earn a pilot's license. Richard Branson suffered from dyslexia before developing Virgin Records and becoming the fourth richest person in the UK. Bethany Hamilton lost her left arm to a shark bite while surfing but hopped right back on her board and won first place in the Explorer Women's Division of the National Scholastic Surfing Association National Championships.

It was the belief that they *could* do it that set them free *to* do it.

There is a spirit-force called faith that functions as a feeder system for self-confidence. With that kind of operating system within us, we are capable of doing anything we put our minds to. We can survive through dire circumstances; we can endure what seems unbearable; we can see what others cannot see; we can elevate ourselves over any obstacles in our way.

We can do all things through Christ.

But faith is not reserved only for those who call themselves Christians. This feeding system is nondenominational; it is an important component of how we were created at birth. Life challenges threaten this natural feeding of our spirits, causing many of us to doubt our innate internal power. But in truth, God did not give some the capacity to overcome and rise and ignore others. Every human on earth has been seeded with the capacity to be more than they believe. We just have to find a way to nourish that seed, pulling the weeds that threaten to strangle it.

I have always believed in the power of faith but I must confess that in difficult times, I have backed away, frightened by forces outside my life that seemed greater than me. But I've had to refocus on that divine seed, planted within us at birth and nurtured throughout our lives by God. Once that relationship is established, once we open ourselves up to the message the Divine has implanted in our DNA, then we *can*, in fact, get over, get up, get out, and get beyond our current circumstances. What God has planted and nurtured cannot be defeated. It may sway and bend during the storms in our lives but it cannot be destroyed.

Whenever I think about the many people who overcame mental and physical disabilities, economic hardships, and racial stereotypes to succeed mightily in life, I am inspired. They remind us of how much we all have been gifted.

We are stronger than the situations that befall us, and we are capable of getting through anything.

Amen and amen.

DAY 90
IN THE TABERNACLE

The Lord is my light and my salvation; whom shall I fear? The Lord is the strength of my life; of whom shall I be afraid? When the wicked came against me to eat up my flesh, my enemies and foes, they stumbled and fell. Though an army may encamp against me, my heart shall not fear; though war may rise against me, in this I will be confident. ...For in the time of trouble He shall hide me in His pavilion; in the secret place of His tabernacle He shall hide me; He shall set me high upon a rock.
—Psalm 27:1–3, 5 NKJV

It is only when we have been able to walk out of a truly bad place that we realize how powerful God's presence and protection really is in our lives.

Anthony Ray Hinton spent more than thirty years in solitary confinement on Alabama's death row for murders he did not commit. The fact that, at the time of the murders, Anthony was around twenty miles away didn't matter to Alabama police. Someone identified him as the killer, and that was all they needed, credible evidence notwithstanding.

On the day Anthony was arrested, he proclaimed his innocence, but the arresting police scoffed and told him that he was "going down" because he was a black man accused of killing three white people. "You're going to jail because you were arrested by white police officers, will be prosecuted by a white lawyer, and tried by an all-white jury before a white judge." Anthony's cry of innocence held little weight. He was going down.

Anthony was tried and convicted for three murders and sentenced to death.

Throughout his incarceration, Anthony held on to God. God knew the truth, and Anthony knew it. On death row, his prison cell was only thirty feet from the execution chamber. Over the years, he watched more than fifty men take that walk past his cell to be executed. His cell was so close, he could smell the burning flesh as electrical current passed through their bodies.

All Anthony had was the firm belief that God knew what was going on and that God heard his prayers. His cell was not made merely of stone and brick but also by poverty, lack of opportunity, and pure racism.

Anthony's story reminds me of Psalm 27: "*The LORD is my light and my salvation; whom shall I fear? The LORD is the strength of my life; of whom shall I be afraid?*" Later, it says, "*In the time of trouble He shall hide me in His pavilion; in the secret place of His tabernacle.*"

Somehow, Anthony Hinton held on to those words, as well as many others, during those thirty-plus years waiting to be executed. He was in prison, yet he was also in God's tabernacle, where he received the gift of God's presence.

To be in God's tabernacle is to be in a place of power. It allows us to recognize and feel God's love. While Anthony was in that cell, he prayed, he reached out to help other men work through their issues, and he laughed. He embodied the beatitude found in Luke: "*Blessed are you who weep now, for you will laugh*" (Luke 6:21). Anthony placed his burden into the heart and hand of God, and after a very long time, he was finally freed, thanks to the work of Bryan Stevenson and the work of the Equal Justice Initiative.

When we find ourselves in dark places, it is tempting to want to give up and believe that the "prison" in which we sit is the end of the story. In those times, we must remember there is the tabernacle, the space where God resides and presides over our lives. In that space, God sees and hears us, God hovers over us like a protective parent. God reaches out and touches us and if we do not move away from that touch, we receive strength for the journey. We have the ability to believe, to hope, to laugh, and, as a prisoner named Paul once said, "*to be content with whatever* [we] *have*" (Philippians 4:11) God's tabernacle is a place where hopelessness can be treated and weakened spirits receive strength.

Anthony Ray Hinton may have been in solitary confinement, but he was not alone. Eventually, he got out of prison, off death row, and away from the forces that sought to kill not only his body but also his spirit. The unjust criminal justice system made Anthony's life miserable, but God stepped in and made sure that Hinton felt the power of God's presence in that dark space. In the tabernacle, God hides us. In the darkest of places, God gives us the light we need to get through and to get out.

You may be in a dark place now. You may be in a place of suffering and oppression and all you can see around you are walls. Wherever you are, I want you to know that all you have to do is look up and know that you are in God's tabernacle. God loves you and is hovering over you, reaching out in the hope that you will reach back so you can experience freedom before actual freedom arrives.

This is the work of resistance. This is the power that has always delivered us. This is the truth that will make you free.

And freedom is God's desire. It is God's will.

Amen and amen.

ABOUT THE AUTHOR

Susan K. Williams Smith is an ordained minister, musician, writer, and activist living in Columbus, Ohio. She has written for the *Washington Post* and *Huffington Post*, as well as her blog, *Candid Observations*. She currently serves as one of the tri-chairs for the Ohio Poor People's Campaign: A National Call for Moral Revival. She also serves as national scribe for the African American Ministers' Leadership Council (AAMLC), and communications consultant for the Samuel DeWitt Proctor Conference, and is the founder of Crazy Faith Ministries. She is a graduate of Occidental College and Yale Divinity School, and earned a D.Min from United Theological Seminary. Her previous book, *Crazy Faith: Ordinary People, Extraordinary Lives*, was published by Judson Press.